M.A. Ogilvie is a research officer at the Wildfowl Trust, Slimbridge, working mainly on goose population studies and the wildfowl ringing programme. His work has enabled him to travel widely in Europe and to make several trips to the Arctic. He is one of the editors of the monthly journal *British Birds* and is on the editorial board of the multi-volume *Birds of the Western Palearctic*. He has written several books on birds and birdwatching.

'Much more than just another birdwatching book. Its purpose is understanding . . . water birds. Its succeeds admirably.'
Waterways News

'There should be a good readership for this book'
The Countryman

'Helpful . . . presented in a fresh mix . . . superb colour plates.'
Wildfowl World

Other titles in the NATURE WATCH series:
Mammal Watching by Michael Clark

(forthcoming titles)
Birdwatching on estuaries, coast and sea
by Clare Lloyd
Butterfly Watching by Paul Whalley
Pond Watching by Paul Sterry

NATURE WATCH

BIRD-WATCHING

on inland fresh waters

M.A.Ogilvie

Hamlyn Paperbacks

BIRDWATCHING ON
INLAND FRESH WATERS
ISBN 0 600 20751 X

First published in Great Britain 1981
by Severn House Publishers Limited
Hamlyn Paperbacks edition 1983
Text © 1981 by M.A. Ogilvie
Drawings © 1981 by Severn House
Publishers Limited

Hamlyn Paperbacks are published by
The Hamlyn Publishing Group Ltd,
Astronaut House, Feltham,
Middlesex, England

Printed and bound in Great Britain by
Hazell Watson and Viney Ltd, Aylesbury, Bucks

Editorial: Ian Jackson and Diana Levinson
Design: Keith Lovegrove

Drawings by Carol Ogilvie

Contents

1 The fresh-water habitat

There are very few birds which make absolutely no use of fresh water, even if only for drinking. Leaving aside the seabirds, which are adapted along with a very few others for living in salt water, almost all other kinds of birds require fresh water or the life that lives in or near it. Those birds more completely dependent upon fresh water for their existence are the subject of this book. They include not just the more obvious waterbirds, such as the grebes and the ducks, but others like the Heron, Kingfisher, Dipper and wagtails. For these birds fresh-water habitat is vital. Yet there is none too much of it, especially in Britain and adjoining parts of northwest Europe, where the pressures on all forms of natural habitat are greatest.

It is, of course, no coincidence that western Europe should be densely populated by Man and by birds. It provides both with a year-round climate that is about the most favourable on the planet. Whereas Man is virtually non-migratory, however, the mobility of birds enables them to maximise their use of the region. Three broad divisions of birds are involved. The first is sedentary, like Man, finding all its needs within the same area. A second group migrates north for the summer, breeding in places which provide all requirements for nesting and rearing of young, but which become unsuitable because of climate and diminishing food supplies in the winter. For them, the relative warmth of western European winters is suitable for the rest of the year. The third group is the least hardy. Mainly, though not exclusively, insect feeders, there are plenty of food and nest-sites for them in the western European summer, but they must leave before the insects disappear in the autumn, and fly south to warmer areas for the winter.

Fresh-water wetlands attract all these birds including some species which actually share characteristics with another group. The Mallard, for example, is resident over much of western Europe, including Britain, but large numbers only winter here, migrating north to breed as far as the Arctic Circle, in Scandinavia and the USSR. Truly sedentary species include the Heron, Bittern and Mute Swan, though exceptional weather, such as prolonged freezing, may induce even them to move away. Winter visitors, breeding well to the north, include many duck species like Teal, Pintail and Goldeneye. Summer visitors are especially numerous and include terns, Swallows and martins and various warblers.

It is immediately apparent, with all these birds dependent to a greater

Figure 1 A winter concentration of Mallard, Mute Swans and Tufted Duck. The birds are so far keeping a small area of water open, but further freezing will force them to migrate south in search of warmer areas.

or lesser extent on fresh water, that birds will always be present in this habitat, though the numbers at some times of year will be greater than at others. The overall mildness of the western European climate, with its general absence of extremes of drought or cold, means that the habitat is a constant one, certainly varying in quality through the year, but rarely if ever disappearing completely, either under frost and snow, or drying up. It is this, of course, which makes the region and its wetlands so attractive to birds, as they can rely on the presence of suitable habitat whenever they want it. This in turn means that the region can support larger numbers and a greater diversity of birds than if much of the habitat was transitory or sparse. On the rare occasions when the habitat does become unavailable, as in severe winters, then the birds do come under great pressures and while some may be able to move away yet further south in search of open water, others perish in large numbers. By the same token, the region can only continue to support the birds it does while the habitat remains in its natural state. The fact that the region is densely populated by Man very greatly increases the demands made on all natural habitats. Wetlands, especially marshes, have been encroached upon most, because once drained they can be transformed into rich farmland. Only the creation of reservoirs and gravel pits, originally to serve Man's ends, has provided any counterbalance to this destruction.

The attractions of wetlands to birds are essentially threefold. Unlike some habitats, they provide not only food and nest-sites but also sanctuary. Apart from the safety of sitting out in the middle of a large body of water, food and nest-sites probably rate more highly for most birds. The animal and plant life living in and around the water make up the food, while most waterbirds' nests are placed in concealing vegetation in or beside the water. This chapter will explore fresh water as a habitat for birds and examine those features which attract them.

An area of fresh water is always exciting with its teeming invertebrate life and abundance of plants growing below, on and above the surface. Even in a small pond, the density and variety of the fauna and flora are difficult to equal. Enlarge that pond to a lake, perhaps with a piece of marsh at one end, and one is in the presence of some of the richest habitat that exists.

Not all fresh waters are as rich as each other, of course. The major controlling factor here is the underlying soil. If this is acidic, with the water coming from granite rocks or from peat, then the water too, will be more acid than alkaline. Far fewer plants and animals can flourish in such water, lacking as it does the basic nutrients essential to support life. Conversely, where the water comes from chalk or limestone it contains plenty of dissolved calcium carbonate. As the alkalinity of the water increases, so does the concentration of dissolved nutrients such as phosphates, nitrogen and ammonia. The presence of these chemicals provides the necessary building material for the microscopic plankton on which invertebrates feed, providing a step up the food chain towards the fishes and the birds.

Fresh waters have been classified on the basis of their alkalinity, or quantity of dissolved calcium carbonate for a given volume of water. One unit of measurement used, the pH, refers to the quantity of dissolved hydrogen ions in the water, which correlates quite well with the alkalinity. A pH value of 7.0 means that the water is neutral; below 7.0 it is acidic, above, it becomes alkaline. However, the pH in any water varies according to the time of year because of the effect of sunlight and temperature and for this reason it is no longer used as widely as it once was.

As well as a system of classification, a series of names has been given to the different and identifiable types of water. The two major types which will mostly concern us here are oligotrophic or acid waters, and eutrophic or alkaline waters. There are some further divisions which will be mentioned briefly later on.

The geology and topography of Britain dictates that the majority of the oligotrophic waters are in the uplands of the north, while the

Figure 2 A dystrophic pool on the edge of high moorland, with stands of bogbean and sedge. The water is acid and peat-stained. While midge larvae are common, molluscs and some other animals are completely absent. The paucity of invertebrates prevents more than a few birds living on such pools.

eutrophic lakes are concentrated more in the southern lowlands. The underlying rocks produce this distribution reinforced by climate, as the plant and animal life of a eutrophic water benefit from a higher input of sunlight and warmth. The birdlife naturally follows the other animal and plant life on which it depends, and so it is the shallower lowland waters of southern Britain which hold far more waterbirds and of a greater variety, than the deep, hill lakes of the north, despite their greater size. However, there is no exclusivity of birdlife to eutrophic waters and many oligotrophic wetlands attract and hold birds which prefer these conditions and eschew the apparent riches of alkaline water.

In the following account of acid and alkaline waters and the main plant and animal communities which live in them, no clear distinction will be made between standing and running waters. There are few birds in Britain which are wholly dependent on running water, and few running waters which are of significance to birds. In the main the streams and rivers of Britain and Europe are too small, or too heavily used by Man, to hold very many birds. It is the standing waters, whether natural or artificial, on which the birds concentrate.

Acid waters, although mainly oligotrophic, can be of another type, called dystrophic. Here the water is not only very acidic and lacking in nutrients, which inhibits plant growth, but is normally stained brown from the peat in the areas where it occurs. This colouring prevents light from penetrating far into the water which further reduces the life that can grow in the lake or pool.

Dystrophic waters are commonest in areas of peat bogland which, in Britain, are largely confined to the north and west. A very few dystrophic lakes occur in southern Britain, and then exceptionally. The dominant vegetation of such waters includes many mosses, especially sphagnum, while typical water plants are bog bean and cotton grass. Insect life is quite varied, with dragonflies and small midges well represented. However, other animal groups, including the molluscs, are generally rare or absent. This combination offers rather little to birds and those species which do use such waters are generally not wholly dependent on them. For example, the Red-throated Diver frequently breeds on tiny dystrophic lochs among extensive bogs in northern Scotland, but the only benefit it derives is safety. It needs a remote and inaccessible site for its semi-floating nest of moss and weed, sometimes but not invariably concealed in a stand of sparse waterweed. The Red-throated Diver finds all its food out at sea or in a much larger, more fertile loch, often many kilometres from its tiny nesting pool. A few ducks, such as Wigeon or Teal, may nest in the surrounding bogs and bring their ducklings to feed on the insects and their larvae in the pools, but there are no concentrations of breeding ducks in such habitat; the food supply would not support them. Black-headed and Common Gulls may also choose to nest in the midst of a wet bog for the safety that it gives from predators such as foxes. Their food, though, will come from far afield.

Figure 3 Wastwater in the Lake District is an excellent example of a steep-sided and deep oligotrophic lake. Few plants grow in it and the shore is kept bare by wave action. Insects and fish are fairly plentiful but there is not enough food to support many wintering birds.

True oligotrophic lakes are a little richer in plant and animal species than dystrophic waters, if only because their water is normally clear. However, nutrients are generally lacking, especially calcium, phosphates and nitrogen. The areas of acidic rocks where they are found lack natural calcium, whether as chalk or limestone. The majority of the natural lakes in the upland areas of Britain and Europe are of this type. In Britain for example, they are to be found in the Lake District and throughout northern and western Scotland. They are often large, and sometimes, especially in hilly areas, very deep, too. Both these physical features affect the life in and around the water.

An oligotrophic lake, particularly one of any size, can be instantly recognised by the virtual absence of any plants growing round the shore. The edges of such a lake are most often stony and bare. In very large lakes, wave action from the wind will erode the shoreline and prevent the establishment of plants, but even in a small area of water of this type, there is rarely sufficient soil or nutrient for a fringe of vegetation ·to form.

This lack of nutrients means that the very bottom link in the ·food chain, the phytoplankton and the zooplankton, are relatively scarce which, in turn, affects the life in all the stages above. Insects and other invertebrate life are more diverse than in dystrophic lakes and sometimes quite abundant, but their distribution within the lake is usually limited by water depth. Few invertebrates can live in very deep water, while shallows, if they exist, may be subject to wave action and so not very attractive. Several kinds of fish live in these lakes, however, especially trout, and if there is a river running out to the sea, sea trout and salmon.

Midges and their larvae are among the most common insects of oligotrophic waters. They are found living in the mud in the deeper water, down to about three or four metres, and on the available vegetation closer to the banks. A small number of different molluscs also live in the mud including the very successful coloniser Jenkin's spire shell. The abundance of invertebrate life in the shallower water is very dependent on the amount of vegetation. In the larger lakes there may be little or none because of wave action, but usually some can survive in the shallower water, well-rooted on the bottom, while in the smaller lakes and ponds there can be quite dense stands. Typical among these are water-lilies, water-milfoils and starworts. One or two species of pond-weed may also occur, though this family is far more typical of eutrophic waters. In these stands of plants live midge and mayfly larvae together with some water beetles and caddisflies. Even on the bare, stony shores there is some life, especially the well-named stoneflies, whose larvae hide under the pebbles and stones, as well as several different species of caddis. Tiny fresh-water shrimps, too, are found under stones along the shore. Where there is adequate shelter and in places where a sufficient deposit of soil has built up, there may be stands of emergent plants, such as bulrush, bottle sedge, horsetail, and common reed, though this last is never in the dense stands found in richer waters.

This combination of restricted animal and plant life obviously greatly affects the birds which can live on or by these waters. As with dystrophic lakes, ducks and waders can breed around them and bring their young to feed on the insects in and above the water surface and also on the seeds shed into the water. There is insufficient food, however, especially in the winter, to support flocks of birds and many oligotrophic lakes are almost devoid of birdlife outside the breeding season and have no great numbers even then. Only the specialist fish-eaters, the Goosander, the Red–breasted Merganser, the Cormorant and the divers, use these lakes regularly all the year round, although again in small numbers.

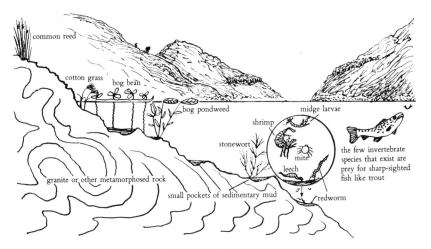

Figure 4 A section through an oligotrophic lake. The clear, acid water is not very fertile and only certain plants and invertebrates live in it. Wave action often results in bare, stony shores. Fish, especially trout, can be quite plentiful, but birds are relatively scarce.

Small insect-eating birds are found around large lakes of this type, though not usually the migrant warblers or swallows. The Dipper, perhaps most often associated with running waters, at least in southern Britain, finds the still waters of large oligotrophic lakes in the north just as much to its liking, where the clarity of the water allows it to search for and find its food on the bottom of the shallows. Pied Wagtails, too, breed and feed round the edges of these lakes, running along the shores and picking up anything live that they can find. Both species nest in holes or crannies or under overhanging rocks and so are not reliant upon thick stands of vegetation for their nest-sites like so many other insect-eaters.

There is a further division of water type between oligotrophic and eutrophic called mesotrophic. Although it can be distinguished from the alkalinity of the water and, to a lesser extent, by the types of plants and animals occurring therein, the birdlife is not very different from that found in oligotrophic waters and so it can be effectively ignored.

Eutrophic waters include most of the lakes and pools in the southern half of Britain and virtually all those less than one or two hundred metres above sea level. The degree of alkalinity naturally varies according to the underlying rock and soil composition and the input of nutrients from the land. The run-off from agricultural land now carries considerable quantities of dissolved nitrogen as farmers put increasing amounts of artificial fertilisers on their fields. Indeed in some areas this has created such a high level of nutrient that algal 'blooms' occur, turning the water green. Exceptionally this can cause other organisms to die off as the algae take up all the available oxygen.

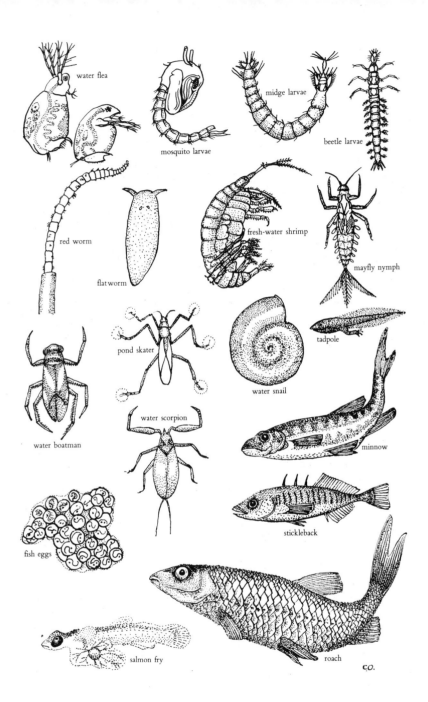

water flea

mosquito larvae

midge larvae

beetle larvae

red worm

flatworm

fresh-water shrimp

mayfly nymph

pond skater

water snail

tadpole

water boatman

water scorpion

minnow

fish eggs

stickleback

salmon fry

roach

c.o.

Figure 6 A typical eutrophic lake with floating and emergent vegetation and a rich growth on the banks. Invertebrate life abounds in the shallow water. Plants and animals support birds of many different kinds and nest-sites are abundant.

Eutrophic waters support a wonderfully rich variety of plants and animals. The basis of this abundance is the plentiful growth of plankton, microscopic or near-microscopic plants and animals, that thrive in the alkaline water. Indeed the life may often be so prolific that its very denseness stops the light penetrating very far, sometimes as little as a metre. The effect of this is to prevent the larger plants from growing in anything but the shallower water. The bottom mud in a eutrophic lake is normally very fertile, promoting algal growth, which in turn provides food for invertebrates which, working up the food chain, feed fish and birds. The variety of the plant life of the shallower water feeds other animals and birds and provides the latter with many nest-sites.

The molluscs are more plentifully represented in eutrophic waters than in less fertile ones. These include a number of species which are a very important food source for diving ducks. The zebra mussel and Jenkin's spire shell, for example, both form important parts of the diet of the Tufted Duck. Crustaceans, too, are abundant, including several species of fresh-water shrimps, on which ducks also feed.

Figure 5 A selection of invertebrates and fish which are present in fresh water and eaten by birds.

Figure 7 The tall bur-reed and the floating pondweed and water-soldier are good indicators that the waters of this lake are fertile and will therefore be visited by a great variety of birds. The seeds of these plants are eaten by Mallard, Teal and Coot.

Birds eat the larvae of a wide variety of insects and those which particularly flourish in eutrophic waters include midges, dragonflies, caddisflies, mayflies, beetles and waterbugs. They are fed upon by the smaller grebes, dabbling and diving ducks, Moorhen and Water Rail, as well as various waders feeding along the shoreline. On hatching, the adults of the smaller insects provide food for birds such as the Swallows and martins, Swifts, warblers and wagtails. Midges and mayflies figure largely in the diet of these birds. The common reed is particularly prone to infestations of greenfly, that well-known garden pest. On the reeds, however, it is taken extensively by Sedge and Reed Warblers, almost to the exclusion of anything else at times.

Figure 8 A Black-throated Diver on its skimpy nest. This species breeds beside large lakes in Scotland and northern Europe. Their legs are set so far back that walking is extremely difficult, hence the nest is always placed at the water's edge.

Figure 9 Red-throated Divers frequently nest in very small pools. In order to find fish for themselves and their chicks they will fly many kilometres to a larger lake or the sea.

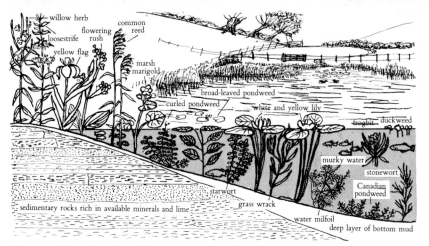

Figure 11 A section through a eutrophic lake. The shallow water is full of available nutrients, and murky from abundant plankton and algae. Rich mud supports lush plant growths in the water and on the bank. There is a wide variety of foods for different birds and of nest-sites in the vegetation.

Among the plants of eutrophic lakes, the stoneworts predominate. These underwater-living, soft even fragile plants, often reach greater depths than other plants and may grow in dense stands. Here they are reached and fed upon by diving ducks such as the Pochard, or obtained by the Mute Swan with its metre-long reach. Many other plants are too tough to be eaten except when young, but their seeds are eaten either directly off the plant, or after they have been shed and are floating on the surface, or lying in the mud. Surface-feeding ducks, like the Mallard, Teal and Shoveler, feed by filtering small items, such as seeds, from the surface debris, or by dabbling at the edges of the water, again sifting out the edible particles from the fine mud. Potamogetons and polygonums are the commonest of these 'pondweeds'. Many emergent plants, or those growing on the edge of the water, shed their seeds into the water where they are found by the birds. These include the large family of sedges, some of the larger grasses, and even a tree, the alder. All these plants grow profusely in the alkaline mud at the edge of eutrophic waters, and only sparsely if at all beside waters which are more acid.

Fresh-water fish, like the other forms of life discussed, become more abundant and show more diversity of species as the water becomes richer. Still waters contain tench, carp, rudd, roach, pike and sticklebacks, while in slow-flowing rivers and streams chub, dace and perhaps barbel are to be found. Faster-running water excludes most of these in favour of trout, salmon, grayling and minnow.

Figure 10 A Little Grebe sitting on its floating nest while four chicks clamber on its back. The chicks beg for food from their parents, pecking at the white bill tip or the white patch at the base of the bill.

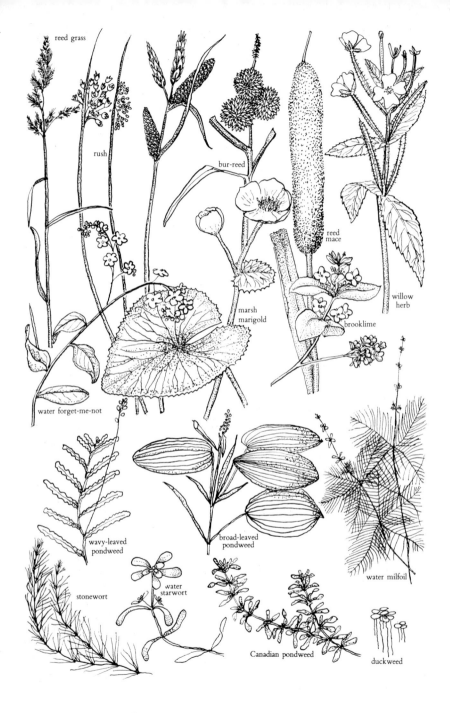

reed grass

rush

bur-reed

reed mace

willow herb

marsh marigold

brooklime

water forget-me-not

wavy-leaved pondweed

broad-leaved pondweed

water milfoil

stonewort

water starwort

Canadian pondweed

duckweed

20

Fish provide the principal food source for the larger grebes, which will take almost any species provided the length is right. The same applies to the Heron and Kingfisher. As fish are more abundant in eutrophic waters, so the birds follow them and one will find more fish-eaters and from a wider range of species on such waters than on acid ones.

We have so far looked at the importance to birds of the food contained in eutrophic waters. It must already be obvious that the abundance of emergent vegetation, particularly the common reed and the sedges, also provides nest-sites for a wide variety of birds, both for those that build their nests actually on the water, such as the grebes and some ducks, and those with small suspended nests, like the Reed and Sedge Warblers and the Bearded Tit. In this way such fertile waters can support birds at all times of the year, providing nest-sites, food for the young, food for the wintering flocks of adults of some species, and total sanctuary for the truly aquatic species.

Having considered fresh water as an overall habitat for birds and shown how the water quality dictates which species of animals and plants and therefore birds, can live there, we can now look at some more detailed points concerning the habitat, which also have a noticeable effect on its birdlife. Why it is, for example, that one eutrophic lake attracts far more birds than another not far away? Why can even an oligotrophic water have a fair variety of birdlife present? The answers usually lie in the detailed topography of the particular lake or pool: the shape of the shoreline, the presence or absence of islands, the amount of shelter and the depth of the water.

There are many waterbirds which will breed readily on islands in lakes. While there are probably none which are exclusively island breeders, the presence of an island, however small, will, without doubt, very greatly increase the probability of several species of bird breeding at a particular water. The advantages of an island are obvious; it provides security against land predators, of which the fox is the most common, though Man comes a close second. Foxes can and do swim, but in the main an island even a metre or so offshore provides a nest-site that is infinitely more secure than anything the bank can offer.

The benefits an island can bring have been well demonstrated by the provision of artificial islands. These are usually quite small, based on the raft principle with oil or large plastic drums as floats, and covered with either bare gravel or tussocks of vegetation. Many species have been encouraged to nest in otherwise bare waters, such as concrete-rimmed reservoirs, including the Great Crested Grebe, Coot and Canada Goose, while on some small lochs in Scotland, the Red-throated Diver now nests safely on rafts, instead of on the bank where foxes or fishermen may cause loss or desertion.

Figure 12 Some of the main food-plants for birds in fresh water providing seeds, leaves and stems for different bird species.

Figure 13 A Canada Goose and a Great Crested Grebe nesting happily side by side on an artificial nest raft. These and other birds can be attracted to breed on gravel pits and lakes lacking suitable natural nest-sites, especially islands.

Even the presence of an island may not guarantee nesting waterbirds, as an island with steep banks is much less suitable than one with gently shelving banks up which birds can walk and young can scramble. One can assess the breeding potential of a newly-dug gravel pit by looking at the shape of any island that may have been left. Active management carried out by conservation groups on such pits has greatly increased the number of nesting pairs of birds by the better shaping of such islands.

Finding a suitable nest-site is one matter and an island may provide several of these, but successful rearing of a brood of young dabbling ducks requires a further topographical feature which varies widely from water to water. Female dabbling ducks normally take their brood of young to a sheltered bay, either of the nesting island if it is large enough, or more usually of the bank of the lake or gravel pit. Here the female stakes out a small rearing area or territory, in which the family will stay for several weeks while the young grow. A bare straight shore is clearly not very suitable for this purpose. The presence of stands of waterweed will provide both shelter and food, but a further important requirement is a small bay or indentation sufficient to provide for a brood of ducklings. The ideal shoreline where ducks will rear their broods is indented like a series of scallops all the way round. Each scallop will then provide a rearing area and a nursery for a brood out of sight of another and therefore not in conflict with it for the available food supply. As with islands these ideal conditions may often not exist naturally, though they can be provided by active management.

The depth of the water is obviously of great importance as it governs what plants will grow and how much life there will be in the water. As already explained, the dense plankton growth in a eutrophic lake may exclude the light from the water much below a metre, limiting plant growth to areas shallower than this. A lake with steep-to banks and water plunging immediately to depths greater than a metre will have little or no plant growth round the edges and so much less shelter and food for waterbirds. This formation is quite common among newly-excavated gravel pits and some reservoirs, but comparatively rare among natural or well-established artificial lakes in lowland Britain. It is more common in some of the oligotrophic lakes of northern Britain, but then these are going to be much less attractive to birds in any case.

It should now be possible to see how an oligotrophic lake with a shelving, well-indented shore, some islands and perhaps a screen of trees around it, will hold many birds, while a bare, newly-dug gravel pit, however fertile the water, may not. The latter, however, is capable of almost infinite improvement as it develops, while the oligotrophic lake's potential will always be limited by the quality of the water.

A birdwatcher approaching a fresh-water area that he has not visited

Figure 14 An aerial view of flooded gravel workings. The shallow pit in the foreground lacks the fringing vegetation of the one behind. Careful planting of the right food and cover plants can attract larger numbers of birds to use such pits. The irregular shoreline and small islands will encourage nesting birds.

before, ought, on the basis of observation of the various features of the water, to be able to predict with some accuracy the kinds of birds and perhaps the numbers that he might see at different times of the year. This knowledge might be thought to destroy some of the point of bird-watching, namely the unexpected, the feeling that almost anything might be seen in any place. While this may be true, the overall pattern of bird distribution is governed by habitat, and birdwatching can be made more rewarding simply because the watcher has some idea of the sort of water he is visiting and therefore why he is likely to see certain birds, and why some will be commoner than others.

2 Adaptations to the fresh-water habitat

The three principal uses to which birds put any habitat are for feeding, nesting and to provide sanctuary. Some species using fresh water take advantage of all three attributes, while others are content with one or two only, finding the others elsewhere. Each species that does use fresh water, for whatever purpose, will show certain adaptations which enable it to feed in, dive under, nest beside, or just about on, water. Such adaptations form the identity of each species. Many share one or more adaptations, but each will exhibit its own unique combination of them.

Feeding

In Chapter I much was said about the wide range of animal and plant foods which are found in the various types of fresh water. Almost every kind of invertebrate and plant can provide food for birds, but clearly rather different birds will eat, say, fish or stoneworts, and equally those birds will require specific adaptations for doing so.

The largest water animals to be taken by birds are fish. These are usually very active and fast-moving requiring specialised techniques for catching them. Most fish-eating birds rely on underwater pursuit, first

Figure 15 The Great Crested Grebe submerges with barely a ripple. It dives two to four metres, staying down for about 25 seconds and coming up head first, eating small prey underwater.

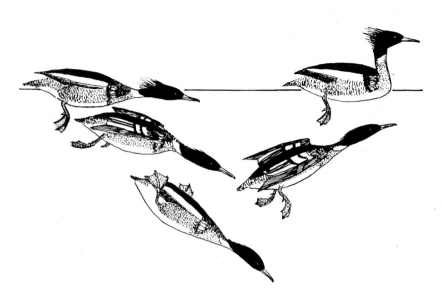

Figure 16 The Red-breasted Merganser submerges easily, though sometimes with a little jump, and is one of the few species to use its wings underwater as well as its feet. It dives to 10 metres or more.

locating their prey and then chasing it and seizing it in their bills. This is the method adopted by, for example, Great Crested Grebes, Red-breasted Mergansers and Goosanders. It requires reasonable clarity of water and hence an absence of dense vegetation. Red-breasted Mergansers and Goosanders find these conditions in oligotrophic waters; the Great Crested Grebe and some of its relatives can hunt successfully in eutrophic areas, despite the less clear water, though they do avoid the thickest stands of underwater weeds. There are, of course, far more fish in such waters, and these birds do not need such large ones to satisfy their needs as the two ducks.

The usual fishing technique of grebes is to sit low in the water, often quite stationary, and then slowly submerge by swinging the head and neck forwards and downwards with the body following. This produces hardly a ripple and certainly no splash which could alarm any fish in the vicinity. Once underwater the grebe uses its eyes to locate a fish before giving chase. All swimming is done with the feet, the wings remaining tight folded to its sides.

Both the Red-breasted Merganser and the Goosander rely on a slightly different method. They sight their prey while still on the surface and then submerge and give chase. Their sighting method is to swim along with their head just submerged, so that they can see the fish under the water. On doing so they dive quickly and swim rapidly after it. It matters much less than with the grebes whether they make a

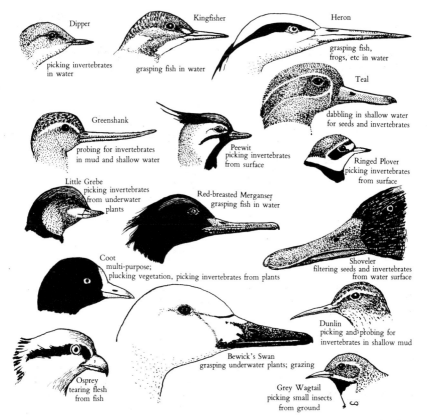

Figure 17 Different bill shapes and the foods for which they are mainly adapted.

splash because the prey is already in sight. Goosanders swim using only their feet, but Red-breasted Mergansers manage to make use of their wings as well; one of the few birds which does 'fly' underwater. Quite why there should be this difference in two closely related birds is not known. Where they live together the main food difference is in the size of the prey, the larger Goosander taking larger fish. No one has studied the true benefits of swimming underwater with feet and wings as opposed to just feet alone.

The Red-breasted Merganser and Goosander have a series of fine serrations along the edges of their mandibles and a slight hook to the tip of the bill; both obvious aids to grasping their slippery prey. Both species may swallow their food underwater, especially if they have dived rather deep, or the fish is small. Normally, though, it is brought to the surface, manipulated into a head-first position and then swallowed. Great Crested Grebes have neither the serrations nor the hooked tip to the bill, but the edges of their mandibles are very sharp to give a good grip on the fish. The grebes also bring most of their prey to the surface before swallowing it, and in the case of sticklebacks and other spiny-finned fish, will spend some time manoeuvring it between their mandibles, breaking down the spines and making the fish easier to swallow.

All three fish-eating species can dive to depths of 20 or even 30 metres, but it seems that they usually find their food only three or four metres down at the most. Normal dives last about 30 seconds, though ones of up to two minutes have been recorded.

As well as fish, which may be up to 20 centimetres long, Great Crested Grebes take considerable numbers of invertebrates, including the larvae of caddisflies and dragonflies, waterbugs, beetles and stoneflies. They also eat shrimps, crayfish, frogs and occasionally newts. Their smaller relative, the Little Grebe, does take some fish, but feeds mainly on invertebrates, and in addition to the foods above, eats molluscs in some quantity. These, of course, are picked off the stems and leaves of under-water plants. This is a feeding technique also used by the diving ducks such as the Tufted Duck and Pochard. Like the Little Grebe, in order to submerge they make a little jump into the air, arching the body and pointing the head down vertically. With this impetus they submerge readily, usually with a slight splash. Underwater, they use their feet, but keep their wings folded to their body.

The dives of the Tufted Duck and Pochard rarely last as long as a minute and are normally less than 30 seconds. Both species can dive to four metres, but generally they concentrate on feeding in water no more than one to two metres deep. Most prey is swallowed underwater, only

Figure 18 The Red-crested Pochard and other diving ducks dive with a preliminary jump and go down to two metres or more before surfacing on a level keel.

feeding raft of Shoveler

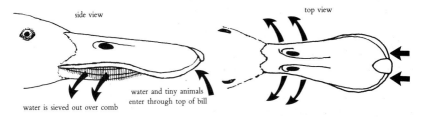

side view

top view

water and tiny animals
enter through top of bill

water is sieved out over comb

Figure 19 The filtering mechanism of the Shoveler, showing how water is sucked in through the top of the bill and squirted out through the sides, helped by tongue action, trapping particles of food in the fine lamellae along the edges of the bill. Groups of Shoveler often feed communally, circling in close packs.

the larger items being brought to the surface. Mixed flocks of Tufted Duck and Pochard are often seen on reservoirs and gravel pits, and it might be assumed that they are feeding on the same items. However, following the rule that no two species occupy exactly the same niche, the Tufted Duck eats mainly animal food, particularly various water snails, while the Pochard feeds on the soft leaves and stems of underwater plants such as stoneworts. When feeding on plants the Pochard often takes in molluscs and other invertebrates clinging to them, while the Tufted Duck will frequently break off bits of plants while attempting to eat a snail. Both species possess bills with cutting edges with a hooked nail at the tip to help in picking up small objects.

There is a whole group of ducks called the dabbling ducks, which includes the familiar Mallard, as well as Gadwall, Teal, Pintail and Shoveler. As their name implies, their principal feeding technique is that of dabbling on the surface or at the water's edge. They move along with their bills just inserted into the water, drawing in the water at the front of the bill and squirting it out through the sides. A series of comb-like serrations along each mandible acts as a filter trapping any seeds and insects which are periodically swallowed. A group of ducks feeding in this way makes a considerable splashing noise which can be heard at some distance.

The most specialised surface feeder among the dabbling ducks is the Shoveler, which has developed a large, spatulate bill. This effectively increases the amount of water which can be sucked in, while the many, fine hair-like serrations inside both upper and lower mandibles work as an extremely efficient filter for even such small particles as plankton. Shovelers can therefore feed in the same area as other dabbling ducks, taking food that is too small for the latter to trap. An additional trick is to feed in pairs or small groups, swimming slowly round and round in tight circles, each bird busy filtering the wake of the one in front. It is thought that this action has the effect of stirring up the water and bringing more potential food to the surface within reach of the broad shovelling bills.

An alternative feeding method for dabbling ducks is up-ending. The body is tilted through 90 degrees and the head and neck stretched down to reach food on the bottom or waterweed growing below the surface. The tail is then up in the air and usually bent over at an angle to maintain balance. The various species of ducks can feed in different depths of

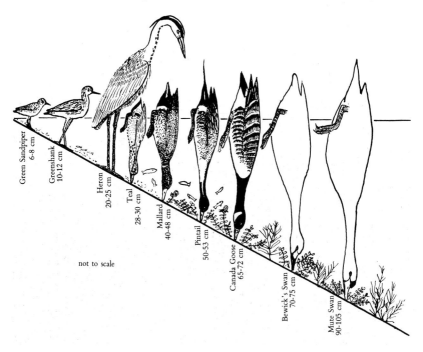

not to scale

Figure 20 A diagram to show the different depths to which species can wade or up-end. This enables several different kinds of birds to feed in one lake without competing with each other.

water in this way, depending on their size and particularly their length of neck. The Teal, being the smallest, is restricted to the shallowest parts, but the Pintail has evolved a much longer neck in proportion to its body size than other ducks, and can consequently reach down nearly 55 centimetres. Each up-ending bout can last five to eight seconds.

A considerable group of waterbirds are relatively unspecialised, being able to feed in a variety of ways on different foods. They can take advantage of many good feeding situations in this way. The three swans, Whooper, Bewick's and Mute, for example, feed on aquatic plants by putting their head underwater and simply pulling them up. In deeper water they up-end, just like dabbling ducks, though with the advantage of being able to reach much greater depths. The Whooper and Mute Swans can both reach down to about a metre. As well as feeding in the water, all the swans are frequently seen out on dry land, perhaps on the immediate banks of the lake or river, but also on farmland many kilometres away. They have learnt, as have many other birds, to graze on grass and sometimes growing crops like wheat and to take the waste left behind after the autumn harvest. The latter consists particularly of spilt grains in barley and wheat fields and the tiny potatoes and broken pieces

Figure 21 Mute Swans feed on the leaves and stems of a wide variety of water plants. Their long neck enables them to reach down underwater further than any other birds. When they have young cygnets they will bring weed up for them from below the surface.

remaining on the surface after harvesting. In this latter respect they are doing the farmers a good turn by reducing the number of rogues which will come up the following year.

Farmland feeding is also the main source of food for wild geese. Some of the smaller species have bills adapted for grazing, with a fairly narrow, pointed shape and a cutting edge along the mandibles. They grasp a blade of grass and sever it with a combined pulling and scissoring action. The larger geese, such as the Greylag and Canada Geese, originally fed by digging for roots and underground tubers with their large, heavy bills. They fed on marshland, probing into the soft mud. This habitat has now virtually disappeared from Britain and most of western Europe and the geese have had to adapt to dry land feeding to survive.

Figure 22 A flock of Whooper Swans grazing on pastureland beside a Scottish loch. All the swan species feed on farmland, including stubble fields and harvested potato fields, as well as grass.

Two birds, the Wigeon and the Coot, will frequently be seen feeding on short grass close to the water, often in considerable flocks. Both species can also feed in other ways, the Wigeon by dabbling and up-ending and the Coot by diving to reach underwater plants. However, grazing is at least as important a method as these alternatives to obtain food. Both species, the Coot in particular, have sharp cutting edges to their bills to help them shear off blades of grass. Although Coot dive for food quite frequently, they are relatively poor divers. Unable to stay down for more than a few seconds, they invariably have to bring their food to the surface to swallow it and only dive in quite shallow water.

As well as the primarily aquatic species so far dealt with, there are many other birds which take their food from the water though they are not necessarily specially adapted actually to live on it. Indeed some of them cannot even swim. Two related species, the Heron and the Bittern, the one quite common and widespread, the other rare and confined to a handful of sites, feed on fish, frogs and newts and the larger inverte-brates. Both adopt the same technique of wading slowly through the shallows until they spot a suitable prey, or alternatively standing motion-

Figure 23 Wigeon grazing on short grass. The leaves are bitten off by the sharp nail at the top of the bill or grasped between the tooth-like lamellae on the sides of the bill and plucked off by a jerk of the head.

less until something comes swimming or crawling past. Whereas the Bittern feeds in dense stands of reeds and is very rarely observed, the Heron is to be seen out in the open, standing like a thin grey sentinel at the edge of the water. When a potential food item is spotted, the Heron can be watched, first of all very slowly stretching down its neck towards the spot, then with a quick drawing back making a lightning stab into the water. The smaller prey is seized between the spear-like halves of the bill, but larger fish are actually speared. It is normal for the prey to be either crushed between the mandibles or beaten on the ground so that it is dead before being swallowed.

Bitterns and Herons both take eels and from these and larger fish can get considerable quantities of slime onto their feathers. To overcome this problem which would quickly lead to a deterioration in the feathers, causing them to lose their insulating and waterproofing qualities, both species have areas of 'powder-down' on their chests and bellies. These are patches of short, thick feathers which produce a fine powder when rubbed. A bird with slime on its head and neck rubs these parts on the powder-down patches so transferring down to the slimy feathers. Vigorous scratching and preening then follows, using specially develop-

Figure 24 Coots give a little jump before submerging, normally descend no more than a metre, and come up horizontally with plenty of buoyancy.

ed middle claws on their feet. These have comb-like teeth along each side which help to clean up the feathers and bring them back into perfect order again.

Two very different bird species have evolved to take fish by plunging

Figure 25 A Kingfisher normally dives from a perch, often submerging completely as it grasps the fish in its bill. On returning to the perch it kills the fish and swallows it head first.

into the water after them, though neither actually swims. The King-fisher dives head-first, usually from a perch, occasionally after hovering, and seizes small fish in its bill. The Osprey flies slowly over the water before hurtling down with half-closed wings, entering the water feet first in order to grasp its prey with its strong talons. It actually appears to dive head-first but at the very last moment before entering the water the legs and feet are thrown forwards in front of the head and it goes in feet first, usually making a considerable splash. Sometimes it manages to snatch a fish from the surface without actually entering the water, but usually it plunges right in and may submerge almost completely for a brief moment. As well as having extremely powerful talons, each claw is lined on the underside with sharp, stiff spicules, like tiny claws themselves, and these ensure a firm grip on the fish as the Osprey lifts it from the water. One final adaptation is that the nostrils can be closed off to prevent water being forced up them as it dives.

A large group of birds, the waders, feed around the water's edge, probing for invertebrates in the mud and between the stems of water plants. The largest flocks of waders are found on the coast, on the mud-flats of large estuaries. A number of species occur regularly by fresh water, however, including flocks of Lapwing and Golden Plover, both

Figure 26 A Heron stalking through shallow water in search of prey. The stealth of their walk is succeeded by a lightning stab of their powerful bill. They regularly take fish up to 100 gm in weight, as well as frogs, newts and large invertebrates.

Figure 27 Bitterns are very rarely seen in the open; this one has emerged into a clearing cut in the reeds. Usually the only indication of their presence is a low, far-carrying booming call.

Figure 30 An Osprey leaving the water with a trout grasped in its talons. The fish is held with the head pointing forwards to reduce wind resistance as the bird flies back to the nest with it.

of which additionally feed widely on farmland, and small numbers, often singles, of the Green Sandpiper, Greenshank and Common Sandpiper. This last is often found beside running water as well as on the shores of lakes and reservoirs. All these species have elongated bills, some very long indeed, and they feel for their food in the mud with the sensitive and slightly flexible tips to their mandibles.

Waders will also feed on visible objects, insects crawling over the mud or swimming on top of the water, and this is how gulls feed on the water, too, pecking at food items as they swim. Their close relatives, the terns, feed more by diving, usually after a preliminary hover to locate their small fish prey. The dive is a rather splashy one, the fish being seized in the bill.

Fresh-water areas are the breeding grounds of myriad small insects. While most of the birds considered so far feed on underwater life, including the eggs and larvae of many insects, once these flies and midges hatch, they provide food for several other bird species. Swifts, Swallows and martins take the insects in flight, swooping to and fro over the water. Warblers do some aerial feeding, flying up into the air in pursuit of a single insect, although they usually work their way through the vegetation, picking the insects off the stems and leaves. Here they join another pecking group of birds, the buntings, especially the Reed Bunting. This species also feeds off the vegetation, but takes seeds and buds more than insects.

The final group of waterbirds are the wagtails and pipits, ground

Figure 28 An Osprey tears with its powerful bill at a fish held in its talons. An adult bird needs up to 400 gm of fish per day and will catch between one and four, depending on size, to satisfy its appetite.

Figure 29 A female Goldeneye emerging from her nest-box high up in a tree. The young when they hatch free-fall to the ground, landing lightly because of their small weight and covering of soft down.

Figure 31 A Common Sandpiper with a small mollusc in its bill. Like other waders with short bills most of its food is found on or close to the surface. It feeds along the sides of reservoirs, gravel pits and mountain streams.

feeders on insects. They can be seen running along the water's edge, in short rushes, bobbing down to pick up an item of food.

Nesting

When siting their nests, birds of fresh-water wetlands make use of the water as a defence against predators. Nests can be floating in the water, attached to plants, or built up from the bottom. Others are placed in tussocks of vegetation in marshy ground, while some species breed in reedbeds and other dense cover growing in shallow water.

The most aquatic species place their nest on the water, building a floating platform. The Great Crested and Little Grebes build such platforms from the stems and leaves of underwater plants which they dive for and bring to the nest. From a distance the nest looks like a flimsy

Figure 32 Birds nesting in or beside fresh water have a variety of nest-sites to choose from. From top to bottom: Coots build their nest up from the bottom in shallow water while grebes' nests are floating, though anchored to plants. The Mallard and most other dabbling ducks nest in dense vegetation. Little Ringed Plovers breed out in the open relying on camouflage to protect their eggs. The Sand Martin excavates a hole in a sand cliff or soft earth bank. The Reed Warbler suspends its nest from reed stems. The Grey Wagtail chooses a ledge in an old wall or creeper overhanging the water, while the Dipper builds under an overhang such as a bridge or arch.

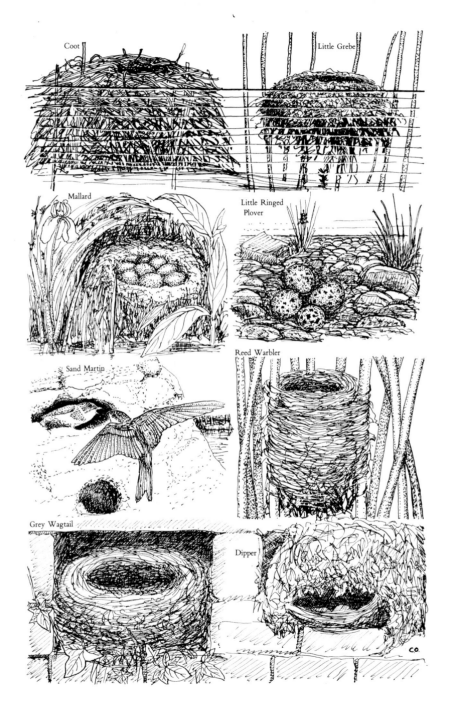

Coot

Little Grebe

Mallard

Little Ringed Plover

Sand Martin

Reed Warbler

Grey Wagtail

Dipper

39

cup projecting only a few centimetres above the surface and liable to be washed away by the slightest wave. In fact every nest is firmly anchored to vegetation, usually reeds or rushes, but sometimes to branches of overhanging willows, trailing in the water. In addition the great bulk of the nest is actually underwater, providing a much firmer base to the shallow nest cup than appears at first sight. An average nest of a Great Crested Grebe can be up to 45 centimetres in diameter at the base and 30 centimetres deep, although above the water it may be only 25 centimetres across and four or five centimetres high. To build such a structure takes the pair, working together, some six to eight days, though they can complete it in less than two. If the weather turns cold or wet, however, while they are building, they will cease operations for a time and might take as long as a month overall.

The Little Grebe builds a nest that is hardly smaller than that of the Great Crested Grebe. In addition it will construct several platforms before finally selecting one as a nest, finishing it off with a shallow cup shape and laying in it. The final cup of a grebe's nest is usually lined with slightly finer material than that of the main structure, though the principal feature of this last stage is the provision of spare leaves and pieces of waterweed with which to cover the eggs. This is done whenever the incubating bird leaves the nest, whether to go off for a brief feed or because danger threatens. Even if disturbed abruptly on the nest, the

Figure 33 A pair of Great Crested Grebes at their nest. Two newly-hatched chicks are riding on their parent's back, safe from predators, while the other parent incubates the remaining egg. Also visible are the lobes on the grebe's toes, the equivalent of the webbing on a duck's foot.

Figure 34 A Little Grebe's nest showing (left) the very conspicuous white eggs common to the grebe family. If the incubating bird is disturbed it quickly covers them with loose weed lying around the nest rim before departing, so that the eggs disappear completely from view (right).

parent grebe will, with a few deft flicks of its bill and head, throw the strands of vegetation over the whitish eggs effectively concealing them from view. It is a perfect camouflage, the rather conspicuous nest contents now an apparent pile of wet and rotting vegetation with no hint of a nest.

Grebes' nests can, of course, get flooded, though generally they will either rise with the water-level or will be built up by the parents to avert the danger of swamping. Heavy wave action such as that caused by power boats is perhaps more of a menace, and grebes have abandoned many rivers and gravel pits for this reason. Another hazard that has to be faced is a falling water-level. Following a sharp drop in the level the nest can be left high and dry and it is usually not long before it is destroyed by a prowling predator.

Coots, Moorhens and some ducks, particularly the diving species whose legs are relatively far back on the body and so find walking difficult, build their nests in the water. These are anchored firmly, either to clumps of vegetation or overhanging branches or to the bottom. While losing the advantage of a floating nest that will rise and fall with changing water-level, they do retain the immense benefit of having a nest entirely surrounded by water and so safe from the great majority of predators. Most of these water-nesting species are capable of rapidly building up the nest in time of flood. The Coot, for example, can add ten or 20 centimetres to the height of its nest within a matter of hours, bringing the eggs up within the cup at the same time. On a much larger scale, the Mute Swan often builds its enormous nest in a clump of reeds or rushes growing out of the water, the bottom of the nest well anchored on the bottom of the lake or canal, and the whole pile rising at least 60 centimetres above the water and maybe twice that down below the surface.

Most of the dabbling ducks do not rely on water to produce a safe site for their nests, but choose instead to find concealment either in vegetation on the banks, or even up to a kilometre away. They are free from the problems of flooding and of keeping the eggs warm in a very damp environment, but have, instead, to contend with foxes, rats and other land predators. Their strategy is to rely on the camouflaged plumage of the incubating female, the brightly-coloured male taking no part, and not even visiting the nest, except perhaps in the first few days of the laying period.

A few waders nest beside fresh water, and they too rely on camouflage to protect their nests. The Little Ringed Plover nests on bare shingle

Figure 35 Aggressive display from a nesting Coot. It has puffed up its feathers and raised up its wings to make itself look larger and more threatening. The nest is built of dead leaves and stems anchored to growing plants.

beside newly-dug gravel pits and makes the merest scrape in the ground as a nest. Its eggs are heavily patterned with black and brown spots on a buff background to resemble stones, while the bird itself has its generally buff and white plumage broken by dark stripes on the head, neck and chest. The shape and therefore appearance of a bird are thus successfully camouflaged.

A well-concealed incubating bird, like a female Mallard deep in a tussock of rushes, will sit very tightly and only flush at the last possible moment, when discovery can no longer be averted. A Little Ringed Plover, sitting out in the open, adopts a different ploy. It will rise and run away from the nest keeping as low as possible as soon as it spots danger, in the shape of a dog, fox or human approaching, even when it is a considerable distance away. By the time the predator or human sees the bird it is well away from its nest. Furthermore the adult bird does its best to lead the predator away from the nest by means of distress calls and perhaps a distraction display. In this latter behaviour the bird may act as if a wing is broken or trailing, fluttering over the ground, calling and all the time moving away from the nest. Dogs have been known to follow such a displaying bird for up to a kilometre, thus proving its efficacy.

A great many species of small birds build a nest suspended in vegetation, keeping them off the ground away from predators and providing concealment from prying eyes. Some species add a further barrier by building their nests in clumps of reeds and other plants actually growing in the water. Reed and Sedge Warblers, Reed Buntings and the rare Bearded Tit all do this. In each case the nest is built of reed stems and leaves or other plant material, neatly woven into a basket-like cup. A number of standing reed stems are incorporated into the structure as it is built. Reed Warblers actually build the main part of their nest between reed stems, taking loops of nest material round them like little handles. Sedge Warblers make their nest a little stronger by bringing the stems through the walls of the nest. The nests are usually built in the previous year's dead stems, so that there are no problems as the plants start to grow. They can sway a great deal in the wind, and occasionally gales will tip out the contents.

Yet another way in which water can protect a nest is demonstrated by a number of hole-nesting species. The Kingfisher, for example, and the Sand Martin, build their nests in holes in earth or sandbanks. Kingfishers usually dig their nest-hole a little way below the top of the bank and almost invariably select a river or gravel pit bank with its base actually in the water. Thus their nest is as inaccessible as possible. Sand Martins nest both in river banks and in quarry faces, and even on piles of gravel washings, and may rely on height for protection rather than water.

Also using holes over water, though not excavating their own, are Red-breasted Mergansers and Goosanders. These species will in addition nest in clumps of thick vegetation, such as heather on the bank. Pied and

43

Figure 36 A Sedge Warbler returning to its nest in a reedbed. The grass leaves from which the nest is constructed are woven round the reed stems so that the stems are completely built into the nest walls.

Figure 37 A female Goosander emerging from her nest in a hollow tree stump. Such a hole, overhanging water, gives considerable safety from predators. Goosanders cannot excavate their own nest-hole but rely on finding natural ones.

Grey Wagtails nest on ledges and small holes in brickwork, so a missing brick in a bridge arch or retaining wall is an ideal place, and if the wall is washed by water, so much the better. Such sites are typical for the Grey Wagtail, though the Pied is more catholic in its tastes and may opt for nesting away from water, in an old garden wall for example. The Dipper, too, frequently nests under bridge arches, wherever it can find a ledge to support its domed nest.

The advantages of nesting in or over water are manifest. The birds have security and concealment from predators and are close to their food sources. Some of the disadvantages, particularly proneness to flooding, have been mentioned. A further drawback, especially of floating nests and those anchored in water, is that the eggs themselves are probably kept cooler and damper than in a land-based nest. The humidity does not matter too much, as a certain degree of dampness is essential for the correct development and hatching of the eggs. The cooling effect of sitting on a pile of damp rushes, however, is harder to correct and it is not in fact known whether the grebes in particular have any special mechanism for counteracting this. One technique they do adopt, along with other species, is the regular turning of the eggs, so that the body warmth of the female is applied equally to all parts of the developing embryo. Incubating birds also have bare areas of skin called brood patches, which are applied directly to the eggs, thus transferring body warmth to them more directly. But again this attribute is shared by most other birds, whether nesting by water or not. The ducks, at least, can provide some extra insulation for their eggs, using their breast down, which they pluck to expose their skin and form brood patches. Whereas other species merely shed feathers for this purpose, ducks line their nests with the soft down plumules and, in addition to thus providing an insulating layer under the eggs, they will draw it over them if they leave the nest for food giving yet more warmth and concealing the eggs from passing predators. The down performs the same function as the spare waterweed which the grebe keeps on the rim of its nest, but the latter can hardly have the same effect of keeping the eggs warm in the adult's absence.

The majority of birds nesting on the ground have young which are sufficiently well-developed to leave the nest within a day, or even hours, of hatching. Birds nesting in water follow this pattern, and all the aquatic species of fresh-water birds have these precocious, or nidifugous, young, as they are termed. There is a necessary penalty of a longer incubation period. In order to produce a greater degree of development before hatching, the egg is often relatively large. However the benefits of producing young which are not tied to a single nest-site for further days or weeks are very great. For a start the parents can take their young to the food, instead of the other way round, as experienced by all species with young reared in the nest. Ducklings, grebe chicks and the young of waders are all running or swimming about freely very soon after hatching, and either finding their own food, or are right on the spot when the adult finds it for them.

The grebes feed their young for quite a long time after hatching, eight

Figure 38 A parent Great Crested Grebe offering a fish to its chick. The edges of the upper and lower mandibles are extremely sharp and so grip the fish firmly. Spiny fins of sticklebacks will be broken off before the fish is swallowed.

to ten weeks, by which time the chicks are very nearly fledged. The adults dive for small insects in the first few days, graduating on to small fish, steadily increasing in size as the young grow. Sometimes an adult will present a fish which is too large for one of its chicks. The latter may attempt to swallow it but when it gives up the adult generally swallows it itself.

A further example of parental care in grebes is that the young ride on their parents' backs, at least during the first two weeks and sometimes longer. They climb up from the tail end, encouraged by the raising of the parents' wings and by calls. Once there they are of course safe from such predators as pike, as well as being warm and sheltered in wet weather.

Ducklings have to feed themselves from the start. The female parent leads her brood to a suitable feeding area, but makes no attempt to pick up and pass on any food items. The ducklings, though, are hatched with well-developed instincts to peck, particularly at small items which contrast with their background. Thus tiny insects and small seeds floating on the surface will be pecked at, initially at random, but gradually with awareness as the ducklings learn what is food and what is inedible. With rare exceptions ducklings do not climb on their parent's back, though small cygnets of Mute Swans do. An important part of their care in the first few weeks of life is regular brooding by the mother bird, especially at night and in cold, wet weather. For this it is necessary for the family to climb out on the bank, and a small island is often chosen as the safest place for this.

The young of Coot and Moorhen share some of the characteristics of both grebes and ducks. They are fed by their parents to start with, but also peck randomly like ducklings, and take in at least some food for themselves from a week or two old. Neither species is able to carry its young on its back, but instead of brooding the young on the bank, they are taken back to the nest for the night. Sometimes special brood platforms are built for this purpose, something that grebes do too.

Physical adaptations

Birds living on or beside water, or obtaining their food from it, show a number of obvious and some not so obvious adaptations to this environment. The most characteristic adaptation is to the foot. All the ducks, geese and swans have webbed feet, with a thin membrane of skin connecting the toes, forming a very efficient propulsion organ. The toes and webbing are compressed on the forward stroke and spread out to give maximum thrust to the water as the leg is pushed backwards. Gulls and terns have completely webbed feet, too, but the grebes and coots have a different method for increasing the surface area of their foot to improve its impulsive effect. They have developed lobes of skin on either side of each toe. As with webbing, the lobes are closed as the leg is moved forward, but open out as it is swung back.

As the legs and feet of waterbirds are immersed all the time, they are a potential source of serious heat loss. A swimming bird is unable to cover its legs and feet with feathers, as do some land birds living in cold climates like the Ptarmigan. What the waterbird does, therefore, is firstly to reduce the blood flow to its legs and feet when the external temperature is low by constricting the arteries. Secondly, by a kind of internal heat exchange, the blood reaching the legs is kept at a much lower temperature than normal body heat. Thus losses to the outside are kept to the absolute minimum.

The mechanical efficiency of swimming with webbed or lobed feet can be improved if they are placed nearer the back of the body, giving much better control and more power. Most waterbirds, and certainly all the ducks and grebes, have their legs well to the rear. This is even more pronounced in the diving birds than those content to swim on the surface. Contrast, for example, the leg position of a Great Crested Grebe with that of a Mallard or a gull. The former pays the penalty, of course, of being a very poor mover on land.

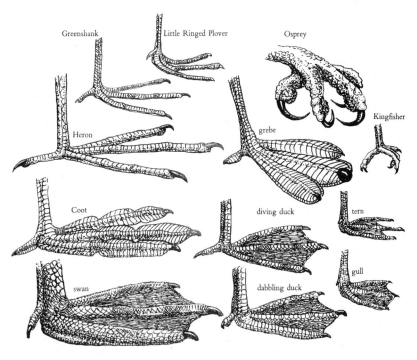

Figure 39 Webbed feet are common among swimming birds like the wildfowl, gulls and terns, but grebes and Coot have broad lobes on their toes instead. For spreading the weight when walking over soft mud, Herons and waders have greatly elongated toes. Both the Osprey and Kingfisher have grasping feet, though only the Osprey grasps its prey in them.

The actual technique of diving requires rather more extensive structural and physiological modification. To be properly effective it is necessary to raise the specific gravity of the bird. This is normally much less than that of water, so that the bird floats on the surface. In order to submerge, and particularly to stay submerged for more than a few seconds, it must be brought up much closer to that of water. Forward movement under the water helps to keep the bird under, but this uses great quantities of energy and even a small reduction in energy expenditure is valuable.

One important modification here is that diving birds have fewer and smaller air spaces in their bones than swimmers. All birds have some hollow bones, many of them linked through special air-sacs with the main respiratory system of the lungs. Such bones make an obvious contribution to lightness in flying birds. Some compromise is necessary, however, if a flying bird also wants to dive. Not only is less air in the bones a good thing, but the bones themselves probably have to be a little stronger to resist the extra pressures of moving underwater, and this too means smaller hollows in the centres.

Diving birds can actually change their specific gravity in two ways immediately prior to diving. Firstly they can exhale air from their air-sacs. Every bird has several air-sacs, mostly arranged in pairs from the base of the neck to the abdomen which together total a greater volume than the lungs. Their function is twofold: to reduce the specific gravity of the bird and to improve the effectiveness of the lungs in ridding the blood of carbon dioxide and replacing it with oxygen. The exact mechanism by which this is done is very complicated, but the advantage of having air-sacs for the diving bird is that it is possible to reduce the volume of air retained in the sacs mechanically. This reduces the bird's buoyancy making it easier for it to go underwater and stay there. Another advantage is that any air remaining in the air-sacs can be utilised for its oxygen content whilst the bird is underwater, thus prolonging the time it can spend there before having to come up for a breath.

The second increase in specific gravity which a diving bird can make is to compress its body plumage, thereby squeezing out most of the air that is normally trapped between the layers of feathers and down. This has the added effect of increasing the streamlining of the bird, so making its underwater progress easier.

Most fresh-water diving birds, as already mentioned, do not normally spend more than two minutes underwater, though some sea-living species, such as the Long-tailed Duck and the auks, may stay down for perhaps twice as long. While underwater they have some control on circulation and heart rate, which directs most of the available oxygen in the blood to the central nervous system and reduces it to the muscles. They are able to tolerate the resulting concentrations of carbon dioxide in their blood and muscles much better than can most mammals. The implantation of tiny electrodes in the heart muscles of diving ducks has shown that in the second or two before making a dive the heart rate increases markedly as does the breathing rate. Then immediately on submersion, the heart rate slows, though it gradually picks up again towards the end of the dive. The bird is clearly making preparation for the dive by increasing its oxygen intake and blood flow.

The birds which dive from the air, the terns, Kingfisher and Osprey, have few if any particular adaptations for actually diving, as they do not remain submerged for more than a second or two. However they do face a problem common to all diving birds of how to see underwater. An eye that sees excellently in the air can be completely useless underwater, unless fairly major adjustments are made. The plunging birds just mentioned seem to make little or no adjustment; they spot their fish from above, dive on the instant and, not infrequently, miss. Certainly they have no ability to pursue their prey underwater if they miss, and so perhaps do not really need an eye that can see to do so.

The birds which swim underwater and chase their prey there, do need to be able to see clearly, and as a result have highly developed powers of accommodation. When a man wishes to focus on something very close to, and then almost instantly on the horizon, the necessary accommodation of the eye is achieved by muscles which alter the shape of the lens slightly, changing its focal length. Diving birds have the same capability, only much more so. Their lenses are rather soft and the muscles controlling them quite powerful. When the bird goes underwater the muscles contract, pulling the lens into a more convex shape, enabling the bird to focus underwater with the very different refracting power that it has compared to the air. The Cormorant, for example, has been shown to have something like four to five times the accommodating power in its eyes of a young person. Diving ducks and grebes are thought to be much the same.

All birds, like many reptiles, have a third eyelid, the nictitating membrane. It lies under the normal eyelids on the inner side and can be drawn across the eye horizontally. It is normally used to clean the eye-ball of dust particles and to keep it moist, also providing an added protection when the bird is in flight and when it is underwater. Although most nictitating membranes are translucent rather than transparent, those of diving birds have a completely transparent central window, through which it is thought they can see quite normally. In addition this window has a high refractive power so that it will bend light rays, even under the water, thus helping to compensate for the loss of normal vision in these circumstances.

The plumage of virtually all birds is waterproof, in that it will shed rain and allow the birds to bathe without getting completely soaked. This waterproofing is largely a function of the structure of the individual feathers, achieved by the tiny barbules which lock together to form the vanes. The preen 'oil' that the birds apply from a special gland above the tail, is not in itself a waterproofing agent, but merely an aid to more

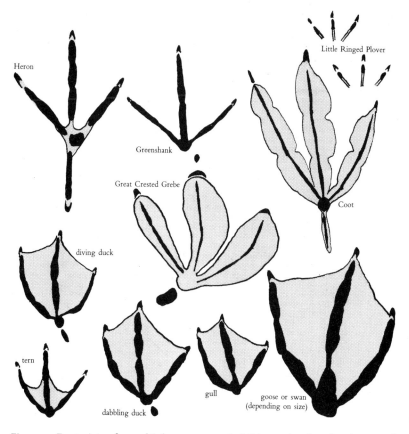

Figure 40 Footprints of waterbirds are commonly left in mud and sand and are another interesting means of identification.

efficient preening, the locking together of the minute hooks along each barbule. Swimming and diving birds have particularly thick, dense plumage, especially the under layers of short down plumules, but this is more for thermal insulation against the cold water than waterproofing, and further adaptation does not seem to have been necessary. Only the Cormorant does not have completely waterproof feathers, at least on its wings and tail. The sight of these birds standing on a rock drying their wings and tail, held spread out, is a familiar one, perhaps mainly on the coast, but more and more inland, on large lakes, reservoirs and gravel pits, as this formerly marine species spreads to these areas. The growth of stocking of fresh waters with trout may be an important contributory factor here.

To close this chapter on adaptations to an aquatic life, we will look at the Dipper, which is unique in its ability to move around and feed underwater. It is a diving bird with a difference. Considerable controversy has raged over exactly how it moves around under the water. It used to be thought that it held on to stones and weeds with its feet. However, a film was taken of the bird in a glass-sided tank showing it using its wings for propulsion and not even touching the bottom with its feet much of the time.

Dippers can swim, though not very efficiently, as their feet lack any kind of webbing, and so they have to paddle very fast to make any headway. They dive not just from the water surface, but also wade into the water and even plunge in from fast horizontal flight. Once underwater the wings are moved strongly out from the body and back again, though not ever fully stretched as in flight. It has been suggested that if the bird were to tilt forward when facing the current in the turbulent streams in which it often feeds, then the pressure of the water over its back would tend to keep it down. However as Dippers can move in any direction relative to the current whilst submerged, this particular aid seems unlikely to be important. The wings are certainly used to keep the bird down, as immediately they cease flapping, it bobs to the surface. It can, if it wishes, take off from the surface of the water. The usual depths of its dives are 30 to 60 centimetres, but depths of 100 to 120 centimetres have been recorded.

Figure 41 Bewick's Swans indulging in threat display. When two pairs are involved, as here, the encounter may go either way. If two families take part the larger one will usually drive off the smaller.

Figure 42 A Mute Swan on its nest with newly-hatched cygnets. After an incubation period of 35 days it will be another four or five months before the young are able to fly.

3 Starting to birdwatch

In order to get the most out of birdwatching in any habitat, it is helpful to be able to identify the birds correctly, to have good binoculars and possibly a telescope, and to be comfortably and discreetly dressed.

Identification of birds comes at the top of every birdwatcher's desires. There is indeed little point in looking at and studying something if one does not know what it is precisely. Good identification books, fitting neatly in the pocket, are readily available; perhaps the main problem is choosing between them. There are three field guides which have become an indispensable part of every birdwatcher's equipment in the last decade or two. The first, and in many ways still the best, is *A Field Guide to the Birds of Britain and Europe* by Roger Peterson, Guy Mountfort and Phil Hollom, published by Collins in 1954, revised since and still in print. It has excellent colour plates with very brief identification pointers opposite, and good texts of about half a page per species with a map. This book held total sway until the appearance in 1970 of *The Hamlyn Guide to Birds of Britain and Europe* by Bertel Bruun and Arthur Singer, published by Hamlyn and still in print. It introduced the new concept of having all the species texts on the page facing the plate. This is undoubtedly far more convenient to use than having to search in two different places, but means that there is far less space available per species. The information is therefore much reduced and condensed. The same format was adopted for *The Birds of Britain and Europe, with North Africa and the Middle East* by Hermann Heinzel, Richard Fitter and John Parslow, published by Collins in 1972, and also still available. The geographic coverage of the book was extended, compared to the other two, but overall it is very little different from the Hamlyn guide in layout and detailed content. It is difficult to advise someone wanting to buy just one book out of the three, as each offers something that the others do not have in information, correctness of the plates, maps or descriptions. Many birdwatchers acquire all three and use each of them at times. If a

Figure 43 Pink-footed Geese taking off from their roosting lake. They will spend the day feeding on stubble and pastures, while the Teal on the lake roost there during the day and feed on farmland by night.

Figure 44 A small flock of Greylag Geese on a lowland lake. This species has been widely introduced to private lakes and gravel pits in several parts of England. Wild birds from Iceland and Scandinavia winter in Scotland and the Netherlands respectively.

poll was taken I think it would agree with my own preference, which is for the Collins *The Birds of Britain and Europe*, just ahead of the Peterson field guide, followed by the Hamlyn guide. To start with, then, buy any one of them, but do not be closed to what the others might be able to offer you.

There are a number of books covering the birds of fresh water in particular but none that need be especially recommended. Those which have an English text to go with plates originally published in eastern Europe are usually not sufficiently orientated to Britain. The identification plates in *Birds of Lake, River, Marsh and Field* by Lars Jonsson, published by Penguin in 1978, are very good and helpful, though the text is sometimes lacking in important information.

There are two books giving details of places to go to watch birds, one general, the other directed solely at all kinds of wetlands. *Where to Watch Birds* by John Gooders, published by André Deutsch and still in print, covers a great many birdwatching sites round Britain, including many inland waters. My own *A Bird-watcher's Guide to British Wetlands*, published by Batsford in 1979, deals with the 100 or so most important British wetlands, in terms of the number of wildfowl and waders regularly found at each. Both include details of how to reach each site, where to obtain the best walks or views and what birds you may see. The wetlands guide gives in addition an indication of the numbers of each of the more important species which occur there.

Good maps are an obvious aid to birdwatching, especially at an unfamiliar site. The latest edition of the Ordnance Survey 1:50,000 scale shows the public footpaths over nearly all the country, and a knowledge of these is a great help when planning the most fruitful walk round an area, as well as avoiding the sin of trespass. Many inland waters are privately owned and access must be sought from the owner. In the case of the numerous drinking water reservoirs, there may be considerable restrictions on entry and where one may go. These barriers to the birdwatcher have been greatly relaxed in recent years with the considerable opening up of reservoirs to public recreation. There are still several closed ones though, and it is essential to obtain the necessary permissions and permits. One's local birdwatching or natural history society will know the regulations for waters in their area. If you are visiting a strange district, information can be obtained from the Water Space Amenity Commission (see Appendix II).

There are a number of wetlands where hides have been provided by different organisations. These prevent the main problem that arises from birdwatching, that of disturbance to what you are trying to watch. If one is out for just a walk, with the additional pleasure of seeing a few birds, then perhaps it does not matter if most of the birds seen are either swimming at the far edge of the lake, or in hasty flight. For more enjoyable birdwatching, however, and particularly if one wants to watch the birds behaving normally, without the stress of obvious human presence, then a more discreet approach is necessary. If one can reach a good vantage point and then stay still for a period, particularly if sitting in the cover of a bush or low tree, the birds gradually cease to regard you as a threat and carry on about their business. Being out of the wind with the sun behind one are nice if they can be achieved.

A good pair of binoculars is the key to any worthwhile birdwatching. For the larger areas of fresh water a telescope becomes a most useful adjunct, though never a substitute. Binoculars come in a variety of sizes, magnifications, and prices. The most useful magnifications are × 8, × 9 or × 10, with the last the strong favourite of most birdwatchers. It is also the most suitable for birdwatching on wetlands where the birds are not always as close as one would like. Nor is the higher magnification the occasional drawback that it is in, for example, dense woodland where one is trying to follow a bird moving fast at fairly close range. Guides to binoculars often make considerable play with the diameter of the objective lens. The diameter, related to the magnification, affects the amount of light entering the instrument and therefore your eye. Nowadays, however, few binoculars are sold which are grossly unsuitable in this respect, and a diameter of 35 to 50 millimetres will be perfectly adequate.

In looking for a pair to purchase, obviously price is a matter of concern, but whereas at the top end of the market one will be buying optics of superb quality for considerable sums of money, the drop in quality does not seem to be related to price as one comes towards the cheaper pairs. For a third of the price of the top-price binoculars one can purchase something very little inferior. A pair, in addition, that one will not be afraid to sling round one's neck and carry around in all weathers. Certainly, as with most products, the very cheap end of the market is to be avoided. Try out several pairs before choosing and avoid any that appear to distort the image, or to have coloured, usually orange or red, fringes round the edge of the field of view or the image. Do look for a pair that sit comfortably in the hands and do not weigh too heavily round the neck or on the chest. For spectacle wearers, many makes have soft rubber surrounds to the eyepieces which will fold down and allow close, but safe contact between the binoculars and the spectacles.

Telescopes are to be thought about more carefully than binoculars. Fewer birdwatchers have one, and one must be prepared to use it far less frequently. Its value cannot be doubted, however, when trying to identify a distant bird, or merely watch in greater detail what the birds are actually doing. A vital addition to any telescope is a firm place to rest it. A tripod is ideal, though something extra to carry, but one cannot rely on a convenient gatepost at every point, or the shoulder of a companion. Nor is lying down with the telescope balanced on a knee very practical in damp conditions, apart from greatly lowering one's viewpoint. At some fresh waters, of course, it is possible to overlook the water from a car, which makes an ideal hide and resting place for the telescope. However there is no doubt that a tripod is best, and quickly found to be essential.

Telescopes, like binoculars, come in a variety of magnifications and there is, perhaps, less agreement between users as to what is ideal. A great many makes, perhaps the majority, have variable magnification, zooming at the turn of a knob from perhaps × 20 to × 45 or even × 60. These have an enormous advantage over fixed magnification instruments as one can scan through a flock of birds on the lowest power and then, on finding something of interest, zoom in to close-up for a really good view. For this, of course, the telescope must be firmly mounted. On a grey winter's day it may be a rare occurrence to be able to use the higher magnifications effectively, above × 50, say, but on the particular occasion, its presence will prove itself thoroughly worthwhile. Even if one is restricted mostly to the lower range of powers, there is still much more flexibility for the user, than if the telescope has only a single magnification, and this should be uppermost when choosing an instrument. Prices vary, though not so widely as for binoculars. Again the advice must be to try out several different makes before making a final selection. Do not rely solely on advertisements, but ask your friends and try out theirs. Telescopes are not light and a tripod adds to the weight. However if one has a tripod, it is easy to place it on the ground, with the legs spread, even if not fully extended, whilst using one's binoculars.

Discreetly coloured clothing is of major importance if the aim is to have the birds at reasonably close range. It is really very surprising how many people out birdwatching wear bright red or orange anoraks and headgear. It is asking a bit much of the birds, which unlike many mammals are able to see the full spectrum, to expect them to take no notice of a vivid patch of colour, however still it stays. This is not to say that it is necessary to indulge in fully camouflaged clothing and darkening the face. If it is vital to be invisible to the birds then a small portable hide is probably the answer. But dull green, brown or grey anoraks and trousers make good sense. Similarly if you want to cover the head, this too should be done in subdued colours. Even reasonably aware birdwatchers sometimes spoil the effect of their sensible clothing by a brightly-coloured woolly hat! Certainly for winter birdwatching clothes should be warm, windproof and preferably waterproof. A lot of enjoyment will be lost if the body is complaining about being cold or wet, or both. For this reason, too, footwear should be stout and waterproof. Wellingtons are the obvious answer unless you are walking long distances and find them unsuitable. At least you can then concentrate on the birds and not worry too much about what you might be treading in.

The birds which live in or make use of the fresh-water habitat can be divided into a number of groups, made up of close relatives. Whilst identification of the detail of species is outside the scope of this book, a general account of each group, where it lives, when one is likely to find it and its principal habits and behaviour, should help to narrow down the field, as well as draw attention to the similarities and differences which occur between and within the groups.

Divers

Three species of diver occur in Europe. Red-throated and Black-throated both breed in north and west Scotland and much of northern Europe, former mostly on small peat and hill lochs, latter on much larger waters. Both, together with Great Northern Diver which breeds in Iceland and Scandinavia, can turn up almost anywhere in winter.

Red-throated Diver

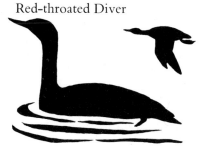

Whilst mainly living on the sea at that time, stragglers wander inland to appear on larger lakes and reservoirs.

Large, heavy-looking birds, about the size of small geese, with longish necks and powerful, pointed bills. Dive smoothly and without fuss, staying under for up to a minute or even more and travel some distance under the water. Feed almost entirely on fish. All three present profile of a bulky bird, but lie low in the water. In flight, a characteristic hump-backed appearance, head and neck stretched out, and feet trailing beyond the tail. All three species make weird, wailing cries on the breeding grounds but are silent in winter.

Great Northern Diver 70–80 cm Largest of the three with shorter, thicker neck and much stouter bill. Identified in summer by its black head; in winter best points to look for are stout bill, thick neck and more peaked forehead.

Black-throated Diver 60–68 cm Grey-headed, with black throat patch in summer and mottled black-and-white back. In winter its fine, pointed bill held horizontally is best distinction from other two species.

Red-throated Diver 55 cm In summer head is grey with vertical black-and-white stripes and red throat patch; back is dark. In winter very similar to Black-throated Diver but the fine bill is uptilted.

Grebes

Grebes divide naturally into three sub-groups. Largest is Great Crested Grebe, which breeds widely throughout Europe on still waters and occasionally on broad rivers; medium-sized are Black-necked, Slavonian and Red-necked Grebes, all three breeding in northern half of Europe and the first two in a handful of places in Scotland and

Little Grebe

northern England; Little Grebe is widely distributed, though avoids high ground lakes. All five can be found in winter on fresh waters anywhere, though medium-sized trio are rare and not often found in more than ones and twos.

Common distinguishing feature is their delicate build. Bills are slender and pointed, heads small, necks, with exception of Little Grebe, quite long and thin. Body sits quite low in water. None of the grebes usually found on waters without plenty of emergent vegetation, and they often skulk in it. Dive for their food, mainly fish and invertebrates, often repeatedly and over long periods, emerging some distance from where they dived. Dives usually accomplished without a splash and barely a ripple, though Little Grebe characteristically gives a little jump before submerging. During the breeding season grebes make a variety of trilling calls.

Four larger grebes develop special ear tufts in summer giving them a very shaggy-headed appearance. In winter their smaller size, and long, thin necks, distinguish them from divers, while general shape and, particularly, their fine bills separate them from the ducks.

Great Crested Grebe 48 cm Unmistakable in breeding plumage with crest and ear-tufts, which in spring are used in striking mutual displays. In winter, large size and white cheeks are prominent.

Red-necked Grebe 43 cm Slightly smaller than Great Crested, with summer plumage of reddish neck and white cheeks. In winter bill is black-and-yellow, while dark crown comes below the eye shading into the greyer cheeks.

Slavonian Grebe 33 cm Reddish breeding plumage, particularly on flanks and neck, is unique. In winter can be told from similar Black-necked by dark crown contrasting with white cheeks and straight bill.

Black-necked Grebe 30 cm Black-necked and headed in summer with golden ear-tufts. In winter dark of the crown merges gradually with whitish cheeks, while bill is always slightly uptilted.

Little Grebe 27 cm Very small and dumpy, lacking length of neck of other species. Generally brown, with chestnut cheeks and throat in summer.

Cormorant

Large (90 cm) black bird, often confused with a diver, having similar low-in-the-water profile. Neck a good bit longer, however, and bill, if a good view is obtained, is straight without the diver's tapering shape, with a distinct hook on the end. Adult Cormorant has yellow patch at base of bill and white face patch. Immature, though, is brownish with

Cormorant

whitish throat and underparts and so much more like diver in winter plumage. Cormorants once confined to sea coasts, but have spread inland and now breed on one or two inland waters and rivers, as well as being found on fresh water in winter. Like divers they fish underwater and slide smoothly beneath the surface.

Heron and Bittern

Heron and Bittern

Two quite closely related species, though of differing habits. Bittern rather scarce, breeding across much of central and southern Europe and in a very few British localities, mostly in eastern part of the country; Heron found all over Europe, and while total British population of some 4,000 pairs is not very large, there are few fresh waters, including quite small streams and pools, where it does not occur. Herons breed in colonies in trees, but range widely for food. Bitterns breed deep in reed-beds and are rarely seen.

Both birds have long necks and legs; seek food by wading through shallow water and stabbing prey (fish, amphibians and invertebrates) with their long sharp bills.

Bittern 76 cm Very secretive; deep booming call may be only indication of its presence. Plumage is brown, mottled with black. If seen in flight, low over reeds, it moves rather ponderously with head held back and legs trailing.

Heron 90 cm Very tall and slender, mainly grey with white head and neck; adult has thin black crest. Head hunched back in flight but long, forward pointing bill and very long trailing legs, together with broad slow-flapping wings are characteristic. Vagrant **Purple Heron** 80 cm very similar in shape but much darker, especially on wings, while close to, rufous neck and chestnut breast are apparent.

Dabbling ducks

Teal

Seven dabbling ducks occur widely in Europe: Mallard, Teal, Wigeon, Pintail, Gadwall, Shoveler and Garganey. Last-named, a summer migrant to Europe. In Britain its breeding sites scattered over southern half of the country. Mallard breeds throughout Europe, but others are confined more to the north, though occur widely in winter. Rather scarce breeders in Britain.

All dabbling ducks can be recognised at a distance by horizontal backs, ending in pointed tail set well above water. Heads generally held close to the horizontal on a fairly short neck. Latter usually tucked down into shoulders, but can be stretched at times of alarm or display. Bills are broad and blunt and relatively large in proportion to head size. All female dabbling ducks are brown, mottled with paler brown, providing excellent camouflage when they incubate their eggs. Males very brightly coloured and consequently far easier to identify.

Dabbling ducks can be seen feeding on surface, with bills just immersed in water, or up-ending, or dibbling in shallows at water's edge. All except Shoveler habitually feed on land as well, flighting out to stubble fields in autumn, usually feeding at night and returning to spend the day loafing on water and banks. Very few fresh waters in Britain without at least a few dabbling ducks.

Mallard 58 cm Male is the most familiar of ducks, with green head, white neck ring, chestnut breast and grey back. A white-edged blue speculum is visible on the wing in flight; brown female also shows this. Female makes the familiar quack.

Teal 35 cm Smallest dabbling duck. Male has chestnut head with broad green eyestripe. Body mainly grey with conspicuous horizontal white stripe above closed wing. Distinctive piping call. In flight, small size, rapid wing-beats and green speculum are distinctive for both male and generally brown female. Vagrant **Green-winged Teal** from North America has vertical white stripe at side of chest in place of horizontal stripe.

Wigeon 45 cm Medium-sized dabbling duck. Male has distinctive chestnut head and buff crown. Grey body shows a white line at rest and conspicuous white forewings in flight. Female differs from other dabbling ducks in short bill, steep forehead, and whitish belly. Speculum is green. Quite vocal birds with whistling calls.

Pintail 66 cm of which tail about 10 cm. Long, central tail feathers of male immediately recognisable, as is combination of chocolate brown head and hind neck, with sharply contrasting white chest and foreneck. Elongated shape and green speculum are obvious in flight. Female is paler brown than most other dabbling ducks with pointed, though not elongated, tail.

Gadwall 51 cm Overall grey male has conspicuous black tail when swimming and is only dabbling duck to show white in speculum in flight. Female has a little white here, too, but is also separable from female Mallard by steeper forehead and whitish belly.

Shoveler 51 cm Broad, heavy bill unmistakable on water or in flight. White chest and chestnut flanks of male are completely characteristic. Both sexes have pale blue forewing and green speculum.

Garganey 38 cm A little larger than the Teal. Male's most conspicuous feature is its white eyestripe, while sharp demarcation between red-brown chest and pale sides also obvious at rest. In flight female shows a pale blue-grey forewing but is best told from female Teal when at rest by whitish throat, white spot at base of bill and more distinctive eyestripe. Far carrying high-pitched croak.

Diving and fish-eating ducks

Commonest diving ducks are Tufted Duck and Pochard, found in winter on almost every lake and gravel pit of any size in Europe except extreme south. In north of Scotland and Scandinavia Pochard is rarer. Tufted Duck additionally breeds over most of northern and western Europe including Britain;

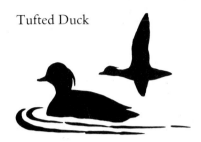

Tufted Duck

Pochard only locally. Other diving ducks of fresh water are Goldeneye, Scaup and Red-crested Pochard. First two breed in northern Europe and are winter visitors further south, including Britain. Red-crested Pochard lives in southern Europe but a few pairs, escapes from captivity, breed in southern England, while another escape, North American Ruddy Duck, has become well established in several areas of the country. Goldeneye has begun to colonise northern Scotland, mainly using nest-boxes erected specially in recent years.

Two fish-eating ducks, Red-breasted Merganser and Goosander, widely distributed on rivers in northern Europe including northern England and Scotland, breed on these and on larger lakes. In winter most resort to the sea, but small numbers occur widely on all types of fresh water. Their small relative, the Smew, breeds in northern Scandinavia wintering to the south in a very few places, with numbers rarely reaching 100, including south and east England.

Common Scoter, a seaduck, breeds on a handful of fresh-water lochs in northern Scotland but more widely in Iceland and Scandinavia. During some winters, small numbers turn up in England on reservoirs and gravel pits. Winter storms can also cause inland occurrences of Eider and Long-tailed Duck.

If dabbling ducks can be told by their straight backs, diving ducks have rounded backs and much shorter tails, held low on water. In general, too, necks are shorter, but this less apparent in a relaxed bird. At closer ranges bills can be seen to be narrower and shorter in relation to size of head. Head itself is more rounded and there is a distinct forehead down to the bill, whereas most dabbling ducks show little or no forehead.

Diving ducks give a noticeable jump into the air before submerging which is a good identification character. Dives are fairly short, but repeated at frequent intervals. Both animal and vegetable matter is eaten.

Female diving ducks generally dark brown all over; males patterned with black-and-white, or grey; not as colourful as male dabbling duck.

Fish-eating ducks also called sawbills; long, thin bills, hooked at the tip the most characteristic feature. Dive freely, often with short preliminary jump, catching fish and free-swimming invertebrates underwater. Males have much black-and-white in plumage; females usually have reddish-brown heads. Shape is rather elongated, with long neck and body.

Tufted Duck 43 cm Male is dumpy, black with bright white side panels, and a short crest. Female is brown, sometimes with white at base of bill and below the tail; white wing-bar shows in flight.

Pochard 46 cm Male is broader in the beam than Tufted Duck, grey backed, grey sides, chestnut head and black chest. Female is dull brown, greyer behind with pale grey wing-bar.

Scaup 48 cm Superficially like a larger Tufted Duck, male Scaup has pale grey back above white flanks. Female has much larger white patch at base of bill, as well as being broader and more heavily built.

Goldeneye 46 cm Male is very conspicuous with white chest and sides, extending up onto the back. Rounded, glossy head has small white spot near base of bill. Female, too, has very rounded head, brown, with no white spot, and pale grey-brown body. Most of inner wing shows as white in flight.

Red-crested Pochard 56 cm Male's reddish head and bill are unmistakable, set on black chest with pale whitish flanks. Crest additionally makes head look very large. Female's combination of brown cap and pale cheek makes it unlike any other diving duck. Both show broad whitish wing-bar in flight.

Red-breasted Merganser 58 cm Shaggy head of male, with long, thin red bill, set on white neck and chestnut breast, very distinctive. Female also crested; lacks sharp boundary between reddish head and white chest of female Goosander. Inner wings show white in flight.

Goosander 66 cm Appreciably larger than Merganser. Male also has green head but lacks crest and chestnut breast.

Smew 41 cm Male is the only nearly white duck; unmistakable with fine black lines on head, chest and back. Female has reddish crown, very white cheeks and grey body.

Common Scoter 48 cm All black male, apart from some yellow on the bill; cannot be confused with other fresh-water ducks. Female has capped appearance but is far darker than superficially similar Red-crested Pochard. No wing-bar on either sex.

Ruddy Duck 41 cm Large-headed, dumpy appearance should be entirely distinctive. Male in summer is ruddy chestnut except for black cap and white cheeks and prominent blue bill. Becomes more like grey-brown female in winter; no wing-bar.

Geese

Several species of geese occur in Europe, mostly coming for the winter. However, Greylag breeds wild in Scandinavia, northwest Scotland

and Outer Isles as well as in feral flocks scattered in several parts of England. Canada Goose introduced from North America, now widespread and common over much of England, especially southern half and also in southern Sweden. Both are resident and can be found on fresh water throughout the year. In northern England and Scotland, wintering Pink-footed Geese and

Greylag Goose

Greylags from Iceland can be found in most lowland areas. Formerly confined to coastal districts, in recent decades they have spread inland, using reservoirs and lochs for roosting on. Can be found during the daytime when they return to water for a drink and a bathe; otherwise spend day feeding on farmland nearby. Flights to and fro at dawn and dusk are in characteristic V-formation.

Geese sitting on water have superficial appearance of large dabbling duck. Back is fairly level ending in a prominent tail, sticking out beyond. Geese, though, have much longer necks, rather round heads and steep foreheads. They are also noisy birds, and a flock is rarely silent for long. On land geese walk freely, their legs being fairly close to the mid-point of their bodies. Graze on land, glean in stubble fields, as well as up-end in water.

Greylag Goose 75–90 cm Grey all over with orange bill and pink legs and feet. Neck is fairly short; head large and rounded. In flight conspicuous pale grey forewings are good identification features. Noisy honking calls.

Pink-footed Goose 60–75 cm Best distinguished from Greylag by overall brown-grey plumage, smaller head and bill, the head being tinged darker brown than rest of body. In flight wings are more even in colour. Higher-pitched calls than Greylags.

Canada Goose 90–100 cm Largest goose in Britain; black stocking neck and head relieved by chinstrap of white. Body is brown; chest paler, forming sharp line with base of the black neck. Neck is much longer in proportion to body than in other geese. Deep, honking calls.

Swans

Perhaps the most unmistakable of waterbirds, these pure white, long-necked and very large birds grace any water on which they occur. Mute Swan found throughout Britain, Ireland and much of northwest Europe except waters on high ground. Whooper and Bewick's

Whooper Swan

both winter visitors to northwest Europe, former from Iceland, Scandinavia and USSR, to Denmark, Netherlands, Scotland, Ireland and north and east England. Latter from Siberia found mainly in Netherlands, southern England and Ireland. All three can be seen up-ending, feeding with just their heads underwater, or grazing on dry land. In flight wings of Mute Swan make musical throbbing sound. Other two species make frequent trumpeting calls.

Mute Swan 150 cm Distinguishing features are orange-red bill with black basal knob, curved neck, and often slightly raised wings. Immatures are brown.

Whooper Swan 150 cm About same size as Mute Swan but appears a little smaller because of more neatly folded wings. Bill is black-and-yellow, the latter descending to a point below the nostrils.

Bewick's Swan 120 cm Not only smaller than Whooper Swan, but neck, head and bill length proportionately smaller compared to overall size. Much less yellow on bill; it never reaches the nostrils.

Birds of prey

Osprey

Osprey 55 cm Only bird of prey in Europe with any claim to be associated with fresh water. Can be confused with nothing else when perched in a tree inspecting the water, and especially not when making its spectacular plunge after a fish. Although confined as a breeding species to northern and central Europe including northern Scotland, birds on passage may drop in, in spring or autumn, at any fertile lake, stay a few days or weeks, and then move on.

Rails

Moorhen

Group includes familiar and very widespread Coot and Moorhen, as well as much less common, and extremely secretive, Water Rail and Spotted Crake. Both Coot and Moorhen can be mistaken for ducks in some circumstances; latter for dabbling duck, former for diving duck. Both, though, swim with distinctive head movement backwards and forwards. In addition, Moorhen perks its tail jerkily up as it moves. On land, long legs of the rails immediately distinguish them from any duck. Coots dive like diving duck, preceded by a small jump into the air, but they dive inefficiently, bobbing up again quickly, even tail first. Small round head and short steep bill, quite unlike any duck's.

Neither Water Rail nor Spotted Crake seen often out of thick cover, in which they skulk, though their squealing calls may be heard coming from the depths of reedbeds.

Coot 38 cm Unmistakable in all black plumage with white frontal shield. Whitish wing-bar shows in flight, which is rather laboured. Sharp 'pinking' cry.

Moorhen 33 cm Like a slim Coot but with red shield, prominent white under tail and thin white line along flanks. No wing-bar in flight. Harsh, unmusical calls.

Water Rail 28 cm Like a small Moorhen but with long red bill, striped flanks and brown back. Undertail area grey not white.

Spotted Crake 23 cm Skulking, but when seen has spotted and striped body and buff under the tail. Bill is short and yellow.

Waders

Wading birds vary quite a lot in size but all share a long-legged, relatively long-necked outline, while most also have a long, thin bill. Characteristically they walk along edge of water, or through the shallows, bending down to peck at items of food. Some walk very sedately, others run on twinkling feet. In flight, move quickly and turn on the instant.

Little Ringed Plover

Rather few waders breed beside fresh water. Both Lapwing and Redshank do so, for example over most of Britain and Ireland, but are also equally at home on fields and meadows away from water. Little Ringed Plovers nest exclusively on bare ground, usually gravel at sides of newly-dug pits. Common Sandpipers breed mainly beside fast-flowing upland streams.

Several species occur on passage at fresh water, and while many kinds, found mainly on the coast, can drop in almost anywhere, principal migrants at fresh water are Greenshank, Green and Wood Sandpipers coming from their breeding grounds of Scandinavia. Snipe are found in marshy areas all year round, and beside open water at times. Oyster-catchers have spread inland, particularly in north of Britain, and while they may nest far from water, do come to it frequently.

Lapwing 30 cm Readily distinguished by overall black-and-white appearance, its crest and lazy looking flight on broad wings. In display flight becomes aerobatic and tumbling and wings make a throbbing sound. Call of 'peewit', its other common name.

Redshank 28 cm Undistinguished bird at rest, grey-brown, with long red legs and reddish bill. In flight, transformed into mainly black-and-white bird as white hindwing and rump suddenly flash into view. Ringing double-note calls.

Greenshank 30 cm Both larger and paler than Redshank, with greenish legs and longer, dark bill, very slightly upcurved. In flight wings are uniformly dark but white rump extends up back into a V.

Green Sandpiper 23 cm Rather dark upperparts, pale underneath, shorter billed than Redshank. In flight has very conspicuous white rump and no wing-bars.

Wood Sandpiper 20 cm A little smaller than Green Sandpiper, not so dark above, though otherwise similar. In flight legs trail beyond tail and it usually gives a distinctive three-note call.

Common Sandpiper 20 cm Dumpy, ever-moving wader, bobbing up and down on a stone or flying low over water. Generally grey-brown, with clear boundary between brown chest and white underparts.

Little Ringed Plover 15 cm Distinguished from closely related, but mainly coastal, Ringed Plover by lack of wing-bar in flight, and thin white line above black forehead. Legs are also paler, less orange.

Snipe 26 cm Long, straight bill held downwards in flight. Overall brown plumage with buff stripes on head and back.

Oystercatcher 43 cm Large black-and-white wader with long orange bill and pinkish legs. Noisy and unlike any other species.

Gulls

Only Common and Black-headed Gulls are widespread inland. Very large Great Black-backed Gull, and slightly smaller Lesser Black-backed and Herring Gulls breed much more commonly round coasts. In winter all five species use fresh water for roosting, and to a lesser extent for feeding and bathing. Flight out for the day to feed on farmland or rubbish tips, and when doing so often adopt V-formation similar to that of geese.

Black-headed Gull

When flying like this, they are not infrequently mistaken for the latter but wing-beats are slow and lazier, nor do they call all the time.

On water gulls ride high, looking very buoyant, a reflection of their flight. Long wings and tail jut out well beyond body and though there is slight resemblance to dabbling duck, length and slimness of gull is quite marked.

Black-headed Gull 35 cm Smallest of our gulls, the summer plumage of chocolate brown head, red bill and legs distinguish it from all others, except major rarities. Black head lost in winter but leaves behind a dark smudge to rear of eye.

Common Gull 40 cm Medium-sized gull rather like a small Herring Gull, but with yellow-green legs and bill, smaller bill and no red spot near its tip.

Herring Gull 55–65 cm Pale silvery grey back, sometimes darker, but never as dark as two Black-backed Gulls. Stout yellow bill has red spot near tip; pinkish legs.

Lesser Black-backed Gull 54–56 cm Similar in size to smaller Herring Gulls. Back very dark grey; bill and legs yellowish.

Great Black-backed Gull 65–80 cm Very large, all black on back, stout bill and pinkish legs.

Terns

This group consists mainly of salt-water species, but some Common Terns breed beside inland waters in Europe and eastern England and Scotland. Black Terns and occasionally other species appear on passage in southern half of Britain breeding widely elsewhere in Europe. Although resembling a small gull, flight is quite different, being

Common Tern

light and airy on slender pointed wings. Beat to and fro, very rarely land on water, and dive, splashily, for food. If they do settle, silhouette is very slim with long pointed tail, and, when on land, very short legs.

Common Tern 35–40 cm Scarlet bill and black tip, all black bill in autumn and winter and red legs, black cap with rest of body greyish and white. Similar **Arctic Tern** is a vagrant inland, but has all red bill, and seen from below, translucent patch in wings towards tip.

Black Tern 24 cm Only tern with all black body and head, relieved only by white under wings. Immatures in autumn have whitish body underneath with black patch on side of breast.

Swallow, martins and Swift

Small birds; highly aerial, rarely settling on ground except to collect nesting material, and Swift hardly even does that. Distribution of all four covers whole of Europe except for the extreme north. All are migrants, only visiting Britain from April/May to September/October

Swallow

time. Swift for shortest period, House Martin for longest.

Swallow and martins, more than Swift, to be seen swooping low over water, seeking insects, while they sometimes actually dip into water, perhaps to take insect from surface, to get a drink, or even to have a wash.

Sand Martin the only species which habitually nests near or over water, though House Martins nest under a few river bridges, and Swallows are often very close. Swifts nest in buildings, often many kilometres from water.

Swallow 19 cm Distinguished from House Martin by absence of white on rump, reddish chin and forehead, and in adult, long tail streamers.

House Martin 13 cm Short-tailed and conspicuously white above, on rump, and below, the entire underparts. Therefore shows white both sides as it twists and turns, unlike Swallow.

Sand Martin 12 cm Brown above, white below, with well-defined brown chest band. Tail is short so that silhouette is like that of House Martin.

Swift 16 cm All-over dark brown bird, with just a faint whitish chin. Best distinction from martins is sickle-shaped wings and relatively much shorter tail. Flight is faster and more erratic. Loud, screaming calls.

Kingfisher and Dipper

These two species need no help in identification; both dependent on water for food. **Kingfisher** 16 cm resident throughout most of Europe, though does not extend far into Scotland or Scandinavia. **Dipper** 18 cm confined to hilly areas of Europe including western and northern England, Ireland, Wales and Scotland. Although found mainly beside fast-flowing streams and rivers, it also lives beside some of the largest lakes in uplands, in whose clear waters it can find its invertebrate food.

Kingfisher spends many hours motionless on same perch, only now and then diving for a fish, or flying fast and straight, low over water. Dipper is much more active species, bobbing on rocks, running down or diving into water, and popping out again back onto the rocks.

Wagtails and pipits

These small birds feed beside water, always in the open and usually on the ground. Grey and Pied Wagtails resident breeders in much of Europe; Pied throughout Britain and Ireland, Grey missing from eastern and southeast England. Yellow Wagtail, a summer visitor from Africa not particularly tied to open water, though liking damp and

Figure 45 A female Mallard incubates her clutch of eggs. She has plucked down from her breast which shows as a rim round the nest. It insulates the eggs from the damp ground and conceals them from predators when the female is off feeding.

Figure 46 A male Canada Goose defends its mate and nest, making itself as large and threatening as possible. Like a Mute Swan it will actually attack humans or cattle that come too close, pecking and also hitting with its wings.

marshy places.

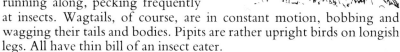

Meadow Pipits, too, nest in wide variety of habitats, but Water Pipit breeds in mountainous areas of southern Europe; a rather local winter visitor to Britain. Has, as its typical habitat, watercress beds on chalk streams of southern England.

All species can be seen walking or running along, pecking frequently at insects. Wagtails, of course, are in constant motion, bobbing and wagging their tails and bodies. Pipits are rather upright birds on longish legs. All have thin bill of an insect eater.

Pied Wagtail 18 cm Only small black-and-white bird with a long tail; adult has black-and-white head; immature is more brown-grey.

Grey Wagtail 18 cm Male is grey above and bright yellow below. Tail even longer in proportion to body than Pied Wagtail's. Black throat patch is good distinguishing mark from Yellow Wagtail. Female is dull grey above and yellow below, with whitish throat.

Yellow Wagtail 16 cm Shorter-tailed and smaller than Grey Wagtail; male has yellow throat as well as rest of his underparts, and is greenish-brown on the back, not grey. Female is paler and duller with yellowish throat and olive back.

Meadow Pipit 14 cm Overall brown in colour with flesh-pink legs.

Water Pipit 16 cm Appreciably larger than Meadow Pipit; grey in plumage tone with dark legs.

Warblers, buntings and others

Small birds of vegetation, to be seen feeding quietly through reed-beds and other stands of plants. Widely distributed; warblers as summer visitors, buntings all year round. In addition a few rarer birds haunt reedbeds, for example local Bearded Tit of eastern and southern coun-

ties of England, the Netherlands and much of southern Europe.

Reed and Sedge Warblers are the only regular breeding warblers of fresh-water vegetation, but other species, particularly, perhaps, White-throats, Willow Warblers and Chiffchaffs, take advantage of abundant food supply of insects to be found there. Small, slim birds, with fine bills; slip quietly through vegetation, rarely coming completely into view.

Figure 47 A pair of Pintail resting in a rushy corner of a lake. Small numbers of this species breed in Britain and western Europe, and large flocks migrate here from the USSR for the winter.

Buntings have short, stout bills for dealing with seeds; their one representative linked to fresh-water habitat is Reed Bunting. It has an upright stance and may be seen feeding on seeding heads of water plants.

Reed Warbler 12 cm Uniform brown warbler, with rufous tinge on upperparts. Best distinguished by its rather monotonous churring song.

Sedge Warbler 13 cm When seen clearly has distinct whitish eyestripe, streaked upperparts and rufous, unstreaked rump. Song is much more contrasting than Reed Warbler's with more squeaky and harsh notes.

Reed Bunting 15 cm Breeding male has distinctive black head and white collar. In winter both sexes are duller brown, but both show white in the tail when flying away.

Bearded Tit 16 cm A tit-like bird though not in fact a member of the tit family, with long tail; rather pale rufous in colour with black-and-white on wings, and on head of male. Best identification comes from the flight call, a metallic 'ping'.

4 What you will see

With the help of the previous chapter it is to be hoped that getting oneself into the right place, with good equipment and some birds to watch, has been made a little easier. The next stage is to discover more about what the birds are doing and why. The following sections go through the various groups of fresh-water species describing some of their particular habits and behaviour and points to look for and to note.

Divers

It is necessary to strike an immediate note of caution concerning divers. If one is in the north or west of Scotland and visiting a water where either the Red-throated or Black-throated Diver breeds or might do so, then it is vitally important not to disturb the sitting bird. Divers desert their nests very readily indeed and many have been forced to do so by the completely unwitting presence of a fisherman, hill walker or bird-watcher. Obviously the accidental disturbance of a nest cannot always be avoided, but on no account should one search for a nest or try to approach one closely having spotted it from a distance.

Notwithstanding the above, there is much that is marvellous and stirring about divers on their breeding grounds, not least the incredible

Figure 48 A Great Northern Diver in breeding plumage, identifiable also by its massive bill and large head set on a short, thick neck. Birds turning up on inland waters in southern Britain are likely to be storm-blown vagrants.

wailing calls with which they establish their territory and communicate between the pair. It is not for nothing that they are called Loons in North America, though unfortunately for us it is the Great Northern Diver, which is not an established breeding species in Britain, which has the weirdest and most thrilling calls. Described in one book as 'uncontrolled idiotic laughter', their wails and screams echo across the landscape. The Black-throated and Red-throated may not have quite the same wild abandon in their calls but they can still be hair-raising if heard through a mist without an obvious source for the noise.

As mentioned in Chapter 2, Black-throated Divers nest on large waters in which they can find ,all their food. Red-throats in contrast select much smaller pools on average, sometimes tiny ones, and fly either to larger lakes or out to sea for food, both for themselves while they take it in turn to incubate the eggs, and later for the chicks. Few studies have been carried out on how far the parents will fly for food, though flights of 10 or more kilometres have been recorded. An interesting series of observations could be made on the distance flown, frequency of feeding of the young and the effect of adverse weather conditions. The first would probably need two people to establish, though the birds fly off conspicuously and could be traced back over a number of days if necessary. The returning bird nearly always advertises its presence by calling as it flies in.

Wintering divers inland in Britain are usually solitary and may be storm-blown vagrants. Sometimes they are picked up dead, from starvation or from some accident, but it is quite usual for a bird to stay on a water for days or even weeks, feeding and obviously putting on weight prior to returning to the sea and, eventually, its breeding haunts. Some indication of diving times for divers was given in Chapter 2 though these were mainly compiled from birds in large breeding lakes or at sea. There seem to be few observations from inland small pools where these solitary birds may turn up in winter. It should be possible to time the frequency of the dives, perhaps in relation to the water depth, if known, and the distance the bird moves underwater. A newly-arrived bird, if not injured or exhausted, might be expected to feed rather more frequently while it recoups its reserves, before settling down to a more steady feeding rhythm after a few days.

Grebes

The very few breeding localities of Black-necked and Slavonian Grebes in northern Britain should not be visited. There are less than 20 pairs of the former and perhaps 60 to 70 pairs of the latter species breeding each year, and both are very vulnerable to disturbance, predation and egg collectors.

Great Crested and Little Grebes are widespread and quite common, however, and can be watched at very close quarters at many sites. And they are well worth watching. The courtship display of the Great

Crested Grebe has been described many times, but always repays watching again and again. That of the Little Grebe is much less spectacular and relies more on calls than visual displays.

When Great Crested Grebes are courting in the spring the pair goes through four distinct, very ritualised ceremonies. Both male and female can take the initiative. The most common display has both birds indulging in head-shaking, with their elaborate ear and cheek plumes raised and spread. They wag their heads from side to side, quite slowly, occasionally breaking off to preen the scapulars. In a second display one bird will dive silently before emerging close to its partner and rearing up in the water, with its head plumes sleeked. This attitude has been com-

Figure 49 The courtship display of the Great Crested Grebe. Both birds have fully erected their beautiful ear-tufts and cheek plumes, and are slowly shaking their heads from side to side. They are also probably uttering a soft ticking call, only audible at fairly close range.

pared to that of a penguin. Meantime the bird on the surface erects its crests and lifts its wings forward and downward to create the impression that it is twice its normal size. It, too, has a likeness, this time to a large, furry cat! These two displays may be suddenly broken into by the third, where one bird lifts itself out of the water and patters away across the surface for several metres before subsiding again, turning and facing its partner and adopting the cat-like posture. Finally there is the so-called weed-ceremony. This is a beautiful and stately performance and occurs when the pair are nearing the time of mating and beginning to build a nest. It starts with them wagging their heads, as in the first display. They then drift apart, rearing up in the water until apparently only supported by their tails. On the same instant both birds dive, to appear a few moments later with bills full of waterweed. They swim together quickly, heads low in the water, then rear up breast to breast and literally seem to dance together. Their feet trample vigorously in the water to maintain their position, while all the time they wag their heads from side to side, still holding the weed in their bills. At this point it is possible to tell which is male and which is female. The male's head is always held higher and his bill swings to and fro above that of the female. The pair subside from the dance, drop the weed and the ceremony is over. It will be repeated several times in the last stages of courtship.

These displays are some of the most elaborate undertaken by any British bird. Fortunately Great Crested Grebes breed on some quite small waters and it is possible to observe their behaviour at close range. They can be put off by the presence of people, but will quickly become

Figure 50 An aggressive encounter between two Great Crested Grebes. With feet and wings threshing the water, they are pushing hard at each other breast to breast. Such fights are quite common in early spring as the pairs establish their territories.

accustomed to them if there is no sudden movement. Look for them, then, on any fertile gravel pit or small lake, where there is plenty of waterweed, both above and below the surface. The peak display time, depending on the weather and latitude, is probably March and April. Once the eggs are laid, the amount of display drops right off, and perhaps the next most interesting occurrence is after the young have hatched.

Great Crested Grebes lay up to six eggs and to start with both parents share the duties of looking after the chicks equally. After about three to four weeks, however, the brood is generally split up, each parent looking after half the young. Surprisingly, this reduces competition between the parents in their search for food, enabling each parent to find more food for the young in its care. Thus one frequently sees a single adult accompanying one or two half-grown or older young. This is not an indication that a parent has died, or that there have been losses of young, merely that one is only seeing half a family.

Little Grebes lack the fantastic courtship displays of the Great Crested, but they do have a very musical trilling note which one can hear rippling out as the birds establish their territories and begin to pair. This begins in September/October time, and there is a further burst of activity in the spring. Most of the trilling accompanies short rushes over the water as a bird defends its territory and tries to drive off an intruder. When displaying to each other the birds of a pair often face inwards, with wings slightly raised and trill vigorously in a duet, turning their heads from side to side.

In winter all five grebe species can be found almost anywhere in the country, but the three rare ones, the Black and Red-necked and Slavonian, are not common in any locality and in some parts to find even one is unusual. Great Crested Grebes are partially migratory and gatherings of a few hundred can occur on larger, very fertile waters, containing plenty of fish. Most British Little Grebes seem to be resident, although some movement takes place in cold weather.

Cormorant

In a few areas, particularly in Scotland, Cormorants have spread inland to breed on wooded islands in large lochs. Further south they have become increasingly common visitors to inland fresh waters, mainly in the winter but also at other times of the year. Their main diet is fish and they have evidently discovered the rich feeding to be had in well-stocked reservoirs and gravel pits. They have come into conflict here with the fishermen, perhaps not surprisingly, as they take fish up to about 20 to 25 centimetres long, including trout, young salmon, perch and other coarse fish. No fisherman seeing this sort of depredation on the stocks that he may well have spent money on building is going to stand idly by. Shooting, the final sanction, is practised at a number of waters, but some success has been achieved by removing, or making less attractive, the perches used by the Cormorants for roosting and for loafing on during the day. They favour buoys, lone trees and some of the artefacts to be found on sailing waters, such as starting boats. If these are removed or draped with netting, it can discourage the Cormorants from staying at that water altogether.

When one does see Cormorants on an inland water, they divide their time between fishing, which they carry out by accomplished diving from the surface, and standing motionless on a perch. It is at this time that they

Figure 51 A Cormorant in the familiar 'wing drying' pose, quite content to use a man-made perch for the purpose. It is widely believed to be literally drying its plumage after a bout in the water but it remains a puzzle why the Cormorant and its relatives should not have fully waterproof plumage like other waterbirds.

adopt the well-known 'wing-drying' attitude. The bird stands upright and opens its wings, holding them out from its body with the wing-tips pointing downwards. The tail is also spread out. It has been widely assumed that the birds were literally drying their wings, exactly as the posture suggested. However, it has always worried some people that any aquatic bird should need to dry its feathers, when in virtually every other species the feathers are waterproof. Indeed the same structure of the feather which renders it waterproof in other species is also a vital part of enabling the bird to fly, and a Cormorant can appear from a dive and immediately take to the wing with ease. In addition, surely a short flight would rid the wings of surplus water more effectively than standing for hours with them outspread?

So what are Cormorants doing when standing like sinister heraldic birds on their perches? The only suggestion to have been seriously considered, but which is certainly not widely accepted, is that the birds are raising their wings in order to balance their bodies. When Cormorants are out of the water they rest on their tarsi, the short leg bones above the feet, rather than on the feet alone. It is thought that this might put a considerable strain on the muscles, especially when the bird has a crop full of some kilograms of fish. If the wings are raised and trimmed according to the wind, they will provide a certain amount of lift, relieving the legs of some of the bird's weight. It is an ingenious idea and has been backed up by the observation that a Cormorant in this attitude is never still, but turns slightly with the wind, opening and closing the wing feathers a little with each puff of wind. While this is probably true, the bird would need to do this anyway if it was drying its wings, just to maintain a comfortable balance.

There is an unresolved problem here, which is well worth some further careful observation. For example, do Cormorants hold their wings out in perfectly still weather when they would get no lift from the wind but could still be drying their feathers? Do they preen in between bouts of wing drying or before starting it? Is the length of holding the wing-drying attitude related to the number of fish they have caught immediately prior to coming out to their perch? These are just a few points that could be studied in order to resolve this interesting question.

Heron and Bittern

The Bittern is a very rare breeding bird in Britain, with perhaps 20 pairs, nearly all in the dense reedbeds of a handful of sites in East Anglia. A sight of one even here is unusual, as they normally stay, skulking, in the thickest cover. With luck one may be seen flying clumsily over the reeds before flopping down again out of view. The most evidence of their presence that one may get is the weird, far-carrying booming call of the male, a low 'thrump'. In hard weather Bitterns often wander far from their usual haunts and have turned up in some very unlikely places where, alas, they usually starve.

Herons, by contrast, may be seen almost throughout the country. They nest in the tops of tall trees, sometimes close to or even over-hanging water, but often enough quite a distance away. In parts of north and west Scotland where trees are lacking, they will nest in low scrub, or exceptionally in marshes and on islands on the ground.

The feeding technique of the Heron, either stalking slowly through shallow water, or standing motionless waiting to stab, has already been described. Herons are, indeed, most frequently seen in this latter motionless posture, but this is not necessarily an indication that they are thinking of food. It is also how they sleep. The most active feeding times, other than when they are feeding young in the nest, is in the early morning and again in the evening. Much of the period in the middle of the day is spent sleeping. To do this the birds have special roosting places where they may often gather in groups.

A Heron roosting site is typically found in the open, perhaps at the edge of a field, but sometimes on a gravel bank surrounded by water, along the bank of a river or among vegetation in a marshy area. Thus if one sees a group of Herons standing out in the open, it is not a sign that they have found an excellent feeding area, but that this is their chosen spot for peace and quiet. Watching at such a roosting site reveals that the birds generally arrive some two to three hours after dawn, coming in singly from a variety of directions, unless there is one excellent feeding site in the vicinity. They drop down and settle, often spending a considerable period preening before going to sleep. Some birds may merely hunch their heads down between their shoulders, while others tuck their bills under their wings with their heads lying over their shoulders.

They will stay like this at the roost, interrupted perhaps by further preening, until late afternoon when they wake, take off, and fly to their

Figure 52 A Heron perched above its nest in a willow tree overhanging the water. Their breeding season starts in early February. They will lay two or three repeat clutches as late as June if their first eggs or chicks are predated or succumb to bad weather.

chosen feeding ground. The roosting sites may be used for several months at a time, but rarely throughout the year. Instead two or three sites are usually frequented at different times of the year; one during the winter, another before and during the breeding season, and yet a third in the late summer and autumn.

Observations on Herons at the nest should be undertaken with great caution as they are prone to desert if disturbed too much, or to abandon eggs or chicks long enough for a predator to move in. Fortunately, however, Herons have a great ability for replacing lost eggs, or even large chicks, re-laying even up to three times. This results in a very prolonged breeding season, with early eggs appearing in the latter half of March, and the earliest young about the middle of April, and birds still incubating eggs at the beginning of July. Hatched eggshells are thrown over the edge of the nest and can be found on the ground at the foot of the nesting tree. Thus some indication of what is happening in the nest above can be judged from this without the hazardous and disturbing climb up the tree.

Swans

The two winter visiting swans, the Whooper and the Bewick's, are often called wild swans as a way of distinguishing them from the resident, and often very tame, Mute Swan. Certainly, with their wary habits and musical trumpeting calls, the Whooper and Bewick's often emphasise their wild nature and the distant tundras where they breed. Yet in recent years both species have adapted to feeding on reserves right in front of hides, so giving birdwatchers and the general public views of them which before were inconceivable. This has been achieved by a combination of complete sanctuary and freedom from all disturbance, coupled with the provision of an abundant supply of grain. Although both species feed principally on aquatic vegetation, they also glean spilt grains from stubble fields and take other seeds, so that this artificial feeding provides them with their normal diet. The two main haunts for Bewick's Swans in England are the Wildfowl Trust reserves at Welney on the Ouse Washes in Norfolk, where over 2,000 have been counted in mid-winter, and at Slimbridge in Gloucestershire, where there has been a winter peak of over 600. At Welney there are also up to 80 Whooper Swans, while a further flock of the latter species lives on another Wildfowl Trust reserve, at Caerlaverock, Dumfries.

With the swans coming in so close to hides and buildings, many aspects of their lives can now be studied that were previously very difficult to observe. This has been helped because it has been possible to identify individuals, both through putting on leg rings, and because the pattern of yellow-and-black on the bills of, particularly, the Bewick's Swans has been found to be individually variable. Visitors are welcome at all the reserves and can see for themselves some of the results of the studies. Of more interest here, perhaps, is to explain what may be happening among swans seen at other places, where they will not allow an approach within many hundreds of metres.

The first thing to notice in any flock of wild swans is that a minority of the birds are in the grey-brown plumage of first-year birds. They do not attain the full white plumage of the adult until they are just over one year old, and even then may have some grey fleckings in the region of the head and neck. Careful observation of the flock will show that the young birds are in small groups of perhaps two or three, together with two adult birds. This is easier to see if the swans are spread out feeding on a field, but can also be observed among swimming birds. What one is seeing is, in fact, a family party of the two parents together with their cygnets. Unlike most other waterbirds, the families of swans and geese stay together as a unit throughout the first winter of the cygnets' life.

When the cygnets hatch, both parents look after them, though neither actually feeds the young which have to find all their food for themselves. As the female has carried out all the incubation while the male stood guard, she needs to feed a considerable amount both to make up any weight she has lost and to prepare for the long migration ahead. The cygnets, too, need to feed as much as possible just to grow. By being in a family unit, both female and cygnets can get on with the job of feeding hard, while the male continues to be the guard, keeping a look out for any predators or other dangers, in between feeding himself. When the time to migrate arrives the family leaves together as a small group, probably within a larger flock, so that the cygnets are physically shown the way to go and also the best stopping places en route. Finally they are brought to the wintering grounds, usually ending up at one or other of the places traditionally used by their parents in past years.

The family bond persists through the whole of the winter, the parents continuing to look after their young, whether keeping watch for predators, or defending them against other swans. Each pair of swans, and more importantly each family, as it feeds either on land or in the water, has an invisible territory around it, into which it tries to prevent other swans trespassing. The territory is quite small, often no more than the length of a swan's neck distant from the bird, and yet it is quite necessary. Swans want to be able to feed undisturbed and not have to compete with other swans for every mouthful. Consequently if one swan comes too close to another, it is likely to be threatened by a peck or a lunging forward, or, more aggressively, the raising of the wings accompanied by calling. Within a flock of swans there will be a fairly well-established 'peck-order', with some swans dominating others in any encounter. A reasonably good, though not universal, rule is that larger families take precedence over smaller ones, and that a family with only one cygnet is still likely to be able to see off a pair and certainly an unmated bird.

Encounters between feeding birds can be observed in any sizeable flock of swans. If one watches a flock carefully, the family parties of two adults and from one to four young will become apparent, moving more

Figure 53 Whooper Swans on a lake in late winter. The flock includes three or four family parties. When the flock is feeding, the larger families will be able to drive off the smaller ones if they get too close.

or less together. If this family party approaches another swan or group of swans, the threat postures, from mild to extreme, can be seen taking place, clearing the moving territory around the family. Sometimes a full-scale shouting match develops, usually between two similarly sized families, or two individuals at much the same level in the peck order. Then all the birds stand around facing each other, raising and lowering their half-opened wings, with heads and necks outstretched, calling loudly. This performance is quite unmistakable and can be both heard and seen at considerable distances.

Because of the strong family bond, it is possible to discover how well the swans have bred each summer. This is quite variable, due to changes in the spring and summer weather on their northern breeding grounds. Both the number of pairs managing to breed successfully and the average number of young in each brood may differ significantly from year to year. In a good season, there will be many families of three or four young, and if enough flocks of swans can be watched and the percentage of young birds counted in each, it may be found that over 30% of the population is made up of birds born that year. Such breeding success will naturally lead to an increase in the total population. However, if the summer has been bad, with substantial losses of eggs or young, then such families as there are may average only one or two cygnets in each, and overall the percentage of young may be no more than 10% or even less.

The resident male Mute Swan adopts a rather different attitude to its offspring. Few birds are more aggressive in defence of their young, charging over the water with wings and feet just beating the surface to produce a most impressive sound, or sailing along with wings uplifted and its neck feathers raised giving it the most imposing appearance. There comes a time, however, usually in the late autumn, when all this changes. On any lake or gravel pit with a family of Mute Swans, the male parent may be seen vigorously chasing his cygnets, which only a few weeks before he was as vigorously defending against intruders. And he goes on chasing them until he succeeds in driving them completely away from the breeding place. They may go together, or be driven off singly. They then have to find their own way around, and, it is to be hoped, eventually end up in a flock of young and non-breeding swans where they will spend the winter.

The point at which the male seems to turn from looking after his young to trying to drive them away, seems to be linked with the changing plumage of the young ones. They start off in a pale grey down which is replaced at a few weeks old by brown feathering. Almost as soon as they are full-grown, in about September or early October, they begin a moult of most of their body feathers, though not of their wings or tail. Gradually patches of white appear, often on the body and flanks, sometimes also on the head and neck. It is this change to a whiter appearance which seems to trigger off the reaction in the adult male parent. Throughout his breeding life he drives off any intruding Mute Swan which lands on his chosen lake. He sees any such visitor as a direct threat to his mate and to his successful breeding. The brown young ones, even when full-grown, do not elicit this response. As soon as they get even a relatively small amount of white on them though, he regards them as intruders and no longer part of his family. Such aggressiveness on the part of the male can cause some people a certain amount of distress as it does appear as if he is trying to kill his own offspring just days after he was looking after them. However it is a perfectly natural part of the swans' life and though it may appear a somewhat drastic method of sending one's offspring out into the wide world it does seem to work.

Figure 54 Adult male Mute Swans are very aggressive in defence of their territory. Any swan landing on the breeding lake will be pursued unmercifully until it flies off again.

Geese

In parts of northern England and in Scotland, large flocks of Pink-footed and Greylag Geese regularly make use of fresh-water wetlands for roosting during the winter months, flighting out to feed during the day on surrounding farmland. They usually leave the water at or just before dawn, the timing linked quite closely to the amount of actual light present, so that they will leave later on a cloudy morning than on a clear one. Greylags usually feed closer to the roost than Pinkfeet, up to six or seven kilometres, as compared with five to 15, and may return during the day for a drink and a bathe which the Pinkfeet rarely do. The Greylags then go out again for an afternoon feed and both species return to the roost as it begins to get dark.

These dawn and dusk flights by the geese are an experience in themselves, particularly if one can position oneself fairly close to the water and on the flight-line which the birds will take. Then as the light grows, so does the clamour of the birds on the water, until there is a mass take-off and with a great roar several hundred geese leave the water and climb into the sky. This may be repeated several times over a period of 20 or 30 minutes before the lake or pond is empty. As the birds lift off so they adopt the typical V-formation so closely associated with wild geese. The exact shape is very variable; it may be a flat V or a very narrow one, there may be roughly equal numbers of birds on either side, or it can be very lopsided. Despite the familiarity of the formation, there is still some dispute as to its exact function.

Firstly the V-formation is not invariable among geese. They can often be seen flying in an ill-defined gaggle. This is most usually the case

Figure 55 Pink-footed Geese taking off from a snow-covered pasture. They will spend the daytime feeding on farmland, returning in the evening to their roost on a fresh-water lake or reservoir which may be up to 15 kilometres away.

when the flock is moving only a short distance, perhaps between adjacent feeding fields or from a nearby field back to the roost. On longer feeding flights, though, and when on migration, the V-formation does seem to be the rule. The main points of contention concerning these formations are whether the same bird leads all the time and whether the geese derive any physical benefit in the form of reduced drag and generally more efficient flying conditions.

If one watches a skein for any period, which is often not easy unless the view around is particularly clear or one can follow the birds in a car, then it quickly becomes apparent that the lead does change as the geese fly. The bird next to the leader may forge ahead and take over, or there may be a change of direction and a bird which was well out on one flank may now find itself at the front. While it is undoubtedly generally true that an older bird or birds will be dictating the direction taken, there is no evidence that the same old bird invariably leads the skein in flight. Like the swans, geese also go around for the whole of the winter in family parties, with the two parents leading their young on migration and looking after them during feeding periods on fields, making sure other geese do not come too close. Consequently any skein of geese is bound to be made up of several family parties, probably with some non-breeders, and because the young birds are used to following their parents, it is likely that one of these will be to the fore most of the time. Although no evidence has yet been found, it is possible that the dominant gander in the group automatically leads them in flight. Such evidence as there is, however, suggests that geese do not arrange their social behaviour like that.

Detailed studies have been made on the subject of whether there is any aerodynamic benefit to be derived from flying in V-formation. Although it is possible to prove theoretically that a group of birds flying in a V do gain, particularly from the lift to be had just behind the beating wings of the bird in front, it is very hard to show that this is in fact what happens in practice.

There are two ways a following body can get help from the one in front. The easiest is to 'slipstream' like racing cars, by getting so close that one is pulled along by the suction effect of reduced pressure just behind a moving object. This might work for cars but for birds there is the added problem of turbulence, the stirring up of the air as something passes through it. And a goose, particularly with its beating wings, creates a considerable amount. Consequently it is very rare to see a bird flying immediately and closely behind another. As the wings flap

Figure 56 Smew winter in small numbers in southeast England and the Netherlands. They breed in holes in trees in northern Scandinavia and the USSR. The very attractive male is shown here; the females are grey-brown with a reddish head and white cheeks.

Figure 57 An adult female Goosander in full wing moult. Like all wildfowl the main flight feathers are shed simultaneously and while new ones grow, a period of about four weeks for this species, the bird is flightless.

up and down they do, however, create a sequence of vortices in the air, swirling masses which can be seen in a different medium behind the oars of a rowing boat. Each of these is a source of potential energy because they come in a series of bumps and troughs according to the wing-beats. If a following bird matched its wing-beats to the bird in front, and kept the correct distance behind, so that as it beat its wings down to give it lift and forward propulsion, it encountered the upsurging air between each vortex, then for one wing at least it would gain some 'free' energy.

That is the theory of it, but when slow-motion film has been taken of skeins of geese, it has not been possible to prove that the individual birds are flying with sufficient precision of wing-beat synchrony and distance to derive the available benefit. There is some dispute as to just how much energy gain is available. It is currently unresolved as to whether even the very modest gain that might be had from flying within fairly wide limits behind and to one side of another bird, and matching the wing-beats more or less but not exactly, would make a measurable difference to the bird following. Clearly on a long migration even a very slight help, reducing the overall effort of flying by a percentage point, might be important. And, of course, if this is so, then there would be a case for the leader changing over at intervals so that each bird could share what benefit was going. Perhaps this question cannot be resolved, short of a wind-tunnel with a flock of trained geese, but it is a fascinating problem. Quite casual observations can show how the geese make use of the V-formation for some flights and not others and how strong winds can affect them, too.

If one needs a simple explanation of why geese adopt the V-formation, then it is because this is the obvious formation to fly in to keep together in a group, yet avoid flying directly behind the bird in front. A goose's eyes are on the side of its head so it can see a bird ahead and to one side very clearly. In addition the rear end of all geese is emphasised by the presence of white feathers, usually at the base of the tail, highlighted by dark feathers in front and behind. It has been shown how the family group is very important for the survival of the young birds, and how family groups combine into flocks, there being safety in numbers. What better way, therefore, of ensuring that the family and the flock stay together in flight than by having some good visual signal, such as a patch of white at the rear end, and flying in such a way that it is easy for the following goose to see it and maintain station without being in the turbulence caused by the bird in front?

Geese returning to the roost, and sometimes when making a landing

---

Figure 58 An adult Coot feeding its young chick. The red colouring of the head and the red bill act as a 'target' for the adult when passing food. As the young grow and begin to feed themselves the red colour fades.

Figure 59 A pair of Moorhens coming together in a territorial dispute. They will interlock their claws and flap hard with their wings as each tries to force the other to give way. Actual injuries, though, are rare.

Figure 60 A flock of Greylag Geese flying in a loose V-formation. This may confer some aerodynamic benefit on the birds or may simply be the most convenient way of flying so that the bird in the front is clearly visible and there is no turbulence.

on a field, quite often adopt a spectacular method of losing height termed 'whiffling'. One moment a flock of geese may be planing down from quite high in the sky, the next they have begun tumbling and twisting downwards, often calling as they fall. What they are doing in aeronautical terms is side-slipping, twisting their bodies and wings sideways so that they spill the air from under the wings and drop more quickly than they could by gliding. The effect is that of a towering mass of falling leaves, apparently out of control, though each bird rights itself perfectly just above the ground. Photographs of whiffling geese have revealed that on occasion they will even twist their bodies upside down, though the head remains the correct way up, the eyes and balancing organs in the ears indicating to the goose exactly where he is in space.

The only goose commonly and widely breeding in Britain is the Canada Goose. It can be found on lowland lakes and gravel pits where it nests, usually in small colonies. In their native North America, Canada Geese usually breed well spread out through tundra and forested regions or along rivers. In Britain, however, where there is a shortage of natural habitat of this sort, they have adapted to breeding more densely to make use of the available habitat. The geese remain territorial and each pair will defend a small area around its nest. The occasional bird will even stand and defend its nest against a human intruder, flapping with its wings and hissing strongly. An alternative strategy is to slip away from the nest and pretend not to be there. When they do this, Canada Geese lie flat along the water, with their head and neck outstretched and only just showing above the surface. For a large bird they become remarkably inconspicuous.

Although Canada Geese defend their nest and eggs against others of their kind, when the young hatch they show much less of a family bond than, say, swans or most other geese. It is quite common to see considerable groups of young Canada Geese in the late summer, perhaps 20 or more, even up to 50, swimming around together in a creche with only a few adults in attendance. These are assumed to be the parents of some of the goslings in the creche, but clearly other parents have left their young by this stage and pay them no more attention. So when one sees three or four adults accompanied by perhaps 20 young ones it does not necessarily means that two pairs have bred exceptionally well and are rearing 10 young ones apiece, but that maybe four broods have amalgamated, but only two pairs have stayed to look after them. The mechanism by which this happens, and what decides which parents stay or leave, has not been completely investigated as yet.

Figure 61 A pair of Canada Geese with their brood. They breed in loose colonies on lowland lakes and gravel pits in England but are less common in Scotland and Wales. They were introduced from North America in the seventeenth century.

Dabbling ducks

There are very few fresh waters of any size in Britain, even the tiny farm ponds and large ditches, which do not have one or several pairs of breeding Mallard. Mallard do not pair for life; instead a new pair bond between a male and a female is forged each year. The process starts quite early, usually in September or October. At this time little groups of Mallard can be seen going through the courting display. Several males gather round a female and pump their heads up and down, calling softly all the while. More elaborate displays often follow including one termed 'head-up, tail-up' where the male lifts its tail out of the water, simultaneously rising up out of the water at the front, so that its head and tail come towards each other. The male may also dip its bill in the water and then flick it out again as it rises up on its tail, meantime producing a sound which can only be described as a grunt-whistle, the name given to this particular display.

The group of males vie with each other for the best position relative to the female, trying to show off to best advantage in front and to one side of her. All of this is aimed at attracting the female to choose one of the males as her mate. This can take quite a while and the displays do not end then. There is a preponderance of males in any normal population of Mallard and in any case even paired males seem prepared to have a go at another female. Consequently a pair of Mallard may find themselves the centre of attention of more displaying males. In this situation the female incites her mate to drive the others off. She ducks her head and bill low, rapidly pointing the bill at the nearest intruding male, quacking urgently all the while. Her mate may try to interpose himself between the female and some of her suitors, but if sufficiently annoyed will rush at the other birds, with its bill open and may even grasp the feathers and have a mild fight.

Courtship displays carry on right through the winter, but may be suspended during cold weather when the birds need to spend most of their time finding food. The onset of warm spring weather will start them off again, however, and a particular feature at this time is the pursuit flights. A small group of ducks flying round will consist of just the one female, usually quacking excitedly, accompanied by from three to 15 males. The flights are started by the female taking to the air, though normally only after she has been pestered on the water for some time. Her mate is not particularly effective at defending her, and indeed it sometimes seems that the pair bond is not all that strong.

In fact the male Mallard only stays with his mate until she has begun laying the eggs and thereafter deserts her. His bright plumage would be a positive disadvantage if he stayed around the nest, of course, drawing the attention of predators to it. The males in an area where there are several breeding pairs gather together when all their females are safely incubating. These loafing groups can be seen in the period prior to their

Figure 62 Four male Mallard 'raping' a female. This is forced copulation often not involving the actual mate of the female. She may have come off her nest to wash and bathe only to be set on by loafing males.

summer moult. They then become secretive and difficult to see, changing their bright body plumage for a dull, female-like brown, and shedding their flight feathers altogether, so that for a time they are flightless.

Few other dabbling ducks breed in Britain in any numbers, and mostly they are seen in winter in flocks. In many areas ducks have a system of flighting out to feed on farmland similar to that of geese, but with the timing reversed. Instead of roosting by night on the fresh water and feeding by day in the fields, they feed at night and roost on the water in the daytime. They can be seen flighting in to roost at about dawn, leaving again for the feeding grounds as dusk falls. This reversal has been put down to the effect of shooting and other disturbance in intensively farmed regions. This habit does help to explain why so many dabbling ducks can be seen during the day just sitting about, sleeping, or preening and bathing. On large refuges ducks may resort to feeding during the day and roosting at night.

Diving ducks

Flocks of Pochard and Tufted Duck can be found on most reservoirs and larger gravel pits in Britain throughout the winter. Tufted Duck have increased and spread as a breeding species in recent years, helped in southern England at least by the great increase in flooded gravel diggings. They are quite late breeders, not laying until well into May and sometimes June. The advantage of this is the much thicker growths of vegetation which will have appeared by then, providing concealment for the nest and, later, the brood. However, unlike earlier breeding ducks where the female can finish rearing the brood before leaving them in order to go off for her annual moult, the Tufted Duck must often desert her young ones before they are fully grown if she is to complete her moult before the arrival of autumn. Thus it is not uncommon to see broods of half-grown Tufted Duck unaccompanied by any adult. They

Figure 63 A mixed flock of wildfowl, mainly Tufted Duck and Pochard. As usual among the diving ducks there are more of one sex present than the other, in this case the males. Pairing in these species does not begin until the spring.

are much better at looking after themselves than dabbling ducks of the same age, so losses at this stage are probably no higher for lacking the mother's protection.

An examination of any flock of Tufted Duck or Pochard will usually reveal an imbalance in the ratio of males to females. This is usually both general to the entire flock present on a particular water and to smaller groups which may be feeding in different parts of the lake or reservoir. It is quite common among birds, such as the ducks, where the pair bond breaks once the female is incubating the eggs, for the sexes to stay apart for some time thereafter. As has been mentioned, Mallard begin to court in the autumn, following the moult of the male and female, which happen at slightly different times and often in different localities. The courtship of diving ducks does not usually start in earnest until the late winter or spring and until this time there is a strong tendency for the sexes to winter apart.

It is rare to find anywhere which has entirely one sex, at any rate in Britain, though there are some nearly single-sex wintering areas in the Baltic region. As courtship is delayed until late in the winter there is no absolute need for the birds to winter together, and there is evidence that the males and females of both Tufted Duck and Pochard have slightly different food requirements which might encourage this. Certainly if one watches a feeding flock of either species, with the birds floating as a loose group on the surface and individuals repeatedly diving so that at any one time perhaps only half of them or less are visible, then it is often the case that males outnumber females heavily or vice versa. What appears to be governing this is that males feed in generally deeper water than females.

This sexual difference can be measured quite easily by noting the position of feeding flocks relative to the edge of the water, and checking whether males generally feed further out than females. In addition the time underwater should be checked as males normally spend longer down than females, averaging perhaps 15 to 20 seconds compared to the females' 10 to 15 seconds. The actual times will be related to the water depths also and may vary from place to place. It is the comparison between the sexes which is of interest at each site. The distance from the bank will only hold true if the bottom shelves fairly evenly from the edge, of course, but the time underwater should vary regardless of location.

Apart from rarities like Ferruginous Duck or Red-crested Pochard, the third most likely diving duck to be seen on inland fresh waters is the Goldeneye. This attractive duck comes to Britain as a winter visitor from northern Scandinavia and generally only quite small numbers, up to 20 or 30, are to be seen at any one site; on many waters, even five is unusual. A very small number of pairs of Goldeneye breed in northern Scotland where they have been encouraged by the provision of nest-boxes. Their normal nest-site is a large hole in a tree but these are increasingly uncommon as older trees die or are felled, and modern forestry management does not permit the development of really old trees, in which holes might appear. The Scandinavians too have had great success in encouraging Goldeneyes to repopulate areas from which they had been driven by the felling of old forests, by providing large numbers of nest-boxes. The idea was first tried in Scotland very many years ago

Figure 64 The spectacular display of the male Goldeneye to his mate. A small number of pairs has begun breeding in northern Scotland in recent years, nesting in boxes specially erected for them near lakes in forested areas.

but it is only in the last decade that there has been any success.

If one is lucky enough to see a brood of young Goldeneye with the mother duck on a Scottish loch or river, it is no use assuming that they have come from the nearest piece of woodland, or even the nearest nest-box if one is visible. For reasons which are not entirely clear, the female Goldeneye leads her brood on a long trek as soon as they leave the nest. The latter event is no easy operation either, as the nest-box or hole may be five metres or more above the ground. After the young have hatched and dried off, usually at about 12 to 24 hours old, the female stands on the ground under the nest and calls them gently. The young peer out of the nesting hole and then, perhaps pushed from behind, tumble down anyhow to the ground. Being light and covered in down they very rarely come to any harm. They then set off on their long walk, led by the female. She may completely ignore the nearest loch or river and distances of over one kilometre have been covered in a matter of a few hours. Losses, of course, do occur, with young getting lost or taken by predators. However, clearly the female thinks that she is taking the young to the best place for rearing them and that this outweighs the dangers of the journey. If one did happen to stumble on a brood being led along a forest path in this way, it would be best to get out of the way quickly, to minimise the disturbance and enable the female to marshal her probably scattered brood again and continue on her way.

Osprey

Although this species only breeds in a handful of places in the north of Scotland the chances of seeing it elsewhere in the country are surprisingly good. In recent years the number of sightings in the southern half of Britain has been increasing, particularly in the months of May and September. Although this increase has been in line with a steady growth in the number of breeding pairs, it is, in fact, more likely that these are birds on their way to and from Scandinavia where there is a much larger breeding population.

The sort of places where Ospreys might be seen on migration are usually lakes and mature gravel pits. The bird is looking for a plentiful supply of fish and much prefers to have a perch in a tall tree close to or overhanging the water. This rules out many new gravel pits and concrete-rimmed reservoirs. It will sit in this perch for hours on end; waiting to see an Osprey make a fishing dive can be a matter requiring much patience. When it does decide that it is hungry then it will take to the wing and fly slowly over the water, sometimes 50 metres or more above it, more usually 20 to 30 metres. On catching a fish, the Osprey will fly with it back to its perch. If this is any distance away the fish is held by both feet, one behind the other, the fish's head pointing forwards. This clearly reduces the drag imposed by the fish. For a very short flight only, or if the fish is quite small, the Osprey will grasp it in just one foot.

Figure 65 The adult male Osprey brings a fish to its chicks in the nest while its mate looks on. The nest can be close to the feeding lake or several kilometres away. The main food is trout.

The Osprey usually waits a little while until the fish is dead, then starts eating it at the head. The intestines are normally discarded. One fish can last an Osprey most of a day; it eats a little, then just sits there holding it, then eats a bit more. If hungry, though, it can devour a fish weighing about 300 grams in about half an hour. A migrant pausing on its way may be quite hungry when it arrives and will attempt to catch a fish several times a day. This can decrease to perhaps once a day, particularly if it is catching large prey. The fish taken will be of whatever species are available, but there is an undoubted preference for trout, though this may be because trout more often live in clearer water and so are more easily caught than the coarse fish, and also come more often to the surface.

Rails

One of Britain's most widespread and adaptable waterbirds is the Moorhen. Probably only it and the Mallard occur on such diverse waters as the largest lakes and the tiniest farm-ponds, as well as being so tolerant of Man that they will live happily on ornamental waters in the centres of cities and towns. Moorhens frequently draw attention to themselves by their noisy squabblings and fights. They are highly territorial, each pair defending an area in which they will not only nest but which must also contain enough food for themselves and their young throughout the breeding season. This territory is sometimes kept for the whole year, but will be re-established or expanded, or a new one created in the spring, usually in March.

The spring is a time of hectic activity amongst Moorhens and because of the need to delineate territories, there are a great many interactions between neighbouring pairs. Even quite small ponds and streams can contain several pairs, each territory, providing the feeding is good, being no more than perhaps 10 by 25 metres in extent, covering both water and an area of bank. An adult defending a territory against an intruder will first utter a sharp call to inform the oncoming bird that it is entering a territory. If this has no effect, a direct attack usually follows with the defending bird running or swimming directly at the intruder, its head held low with its red frontal shield conspicuous against the black head feathers behind. The wings will be raised as will the tail. The latter, indeed, is raised at almost all times, whether in aggression, courtship or if alarmed. It is flicked up and down, greatly emphasising the two large white patches underneath.

The displaying of the red frontal shield is also a feature of minor skirmishing within winter flocks, when birds are trying to keep others at a reasonable distance so that they can feed undisturbed. It has been found that there is a pecking order within such flocks directly related to the size of the red shield; the larger the amount of red, the more dominant the bird. Once territories are established, though, the shield size may not be quite so important.

To return to the territorial dispute, if the charge of the defending bird

Figure 66 A pair of copulating Moorhens are watched by a well-grown youngster. Young first-brood Moorhens frequently help their parents rear the young of the second breed, feeding and looking after them.

does not have an immediate effect, it will rise up on the water or land and open its wings, beating them vigorously, though without attempting to take flight. This usually has the effect of causing the intruder to retreat, it too normally opening its wings as it goes.

Once the territory is established it has to be maintained, and disputes on the boundaries with neighbouring territory-holders are very common. The birds are now more equally matched than when a trespasser is actually being evicted from a territory, and each displays as a mirror-image of the other. At times both the male and female of each pair join in and one can watch four birds actively displaying at each other. On encounter, the rival birds first stand breast to breast, drawn up to their full height. If neither will turn away a fight then develops, the birds sitting back on their tails and grappling with their claws, striking at the other's breast, all the while flapping the wings violently. The two birds will even rise up to a metre off the ground in their struggles, claws locked together, wings beating madly. If they are on the water, then it seems as if one is trying to drag the other under the surface, though this hardly ever actually happens. The fights are broken off as suddenly as they start, both birds retreating, with heads low, tails cocked and flashing the white underside, looking back over their shoulders as if daring the other to start it all over again.

Moorhens and Coots normally rear two or even three broods of

Figure 67 Coots flocking on an icy pool. Winter flocks in Britain often include many migrants from the continent as well as birds that have bred in Britain. The latter rarely migrate except in the severest winters.

young in a year. They start breeding quite early, with eggs laid in March, and carry on through the summer. Indeed in town parks where there is ample food all the year, they can breed in almost every month, though few young probably survive. It is a feature of both species, though more particularly Moorhens, that the young of the first brood help to rear the second. Coots frequently drive off their young when they are fledged, but sometimes they are tolerated within the nesting territory while the parents get on with incubating a second clutch of eggs. Moorhens are so tolerant of their first brood of young that they have even been recorded as incubating the eggs and helping to repair the nest. It is thus quite usual to see a brood of tiny Moorhen or Coot chicks being fed and looked after not just by two adult birds but also by birds in obviously immature plumage.

Although Moorhens are quite frequently seen in small flocks in winter, large flocks of Coot are normal. This species breeds over most of Britain, but the bulk of the wintering flocks are immigrants from the continent. Ringing has shown that they come from as far away as the western Soviet Union. Their different feeding methods, of diving for underwater plants and invertebrates as well as grazing on the banks, are described in Chapter 2. They are also adept at letting other species help them obtain food. It is not uncommon to see a number of Coot swimming closely around a flock of up-ending swans, or paddling round the fringes of a flock of Tufted Duck or Pochard. The swans and diving ducks frequently break-off more bits of plant than they can swallow immediately and the Coot are quick to seize upon these before the other birds can. Thus they allow the ducks and swans to do the hard work underwater for them and obtain virtually free meals.

Waders

Those waders which breed beside water, the Little Ringed Plover and Common Sandpiper, or in damp, marshy places which are often, though not invariably close to open water, the Lapwing, Redshank and Snipe, all have quite noisy and conspicuous displays during their courtship

Figure 68 The display flight of the Redshank. It utters loud, piping calls as it flies on stiffly held wings, first attracting a mate and then conveying to other Redshanks the existence of its breeding territory.

period. In most species this involves the pair flying round, calling loudly, and drawing attention to themselves. Redshank fly in a special way with wings held out fairly stiffly and quivering all the time as well as producing continuous far-carrying, piping calls. Lapwings perform skilful aerobatics, tumbling and twisting through the air, calling their alternative name 'pee-wit', with the emphasis on the second syllable. As they fly their wings also make a considerable tearing noise through the air, from which the name Lapwing comes.

The most curious sound to be heard around a wetland in spring is probably the drumming of the Snipe. The displaying birds dive from a height of 30 metres or more, with their outer tail feathers held out stiffly, away from the rest of the tail. The wind rushing past these feathers produces a strange bleating noise, a kind of musical whirring. It was originally thought that the birds made the sound vocally, that it was a kind of song. But after much debate a very simple experiment was carried out. The two stiff tail feathers were stuck at an angle into a cork attached to a length of string. Then the cork was whirled around the experimenter's head. It produced exactly the sound made by the displaying Snipe. A second, characteristic call of Snipe in the spring is a 'chip-per, chip-per' rhythmic call, usually uttered by the bird sitting on the ground, or standing on a post, though occasionally in flight.

The Little Ringed Plover and Common Sandpiper both have pursuit flights, one bird, usually the male, chasing the female at high speed, and mostly at low level. The Little Ringed Plovers indulge in this display a good deal and it is a very good sign that a pair are thinking of nesting at that site. On the continent, Little Ringed Plovers breed on shingle banks in rivers and sometimes on the coast. In Britain, however, they are more or less confined to man-made excavations, in particular gravel pits, but also industrial waste tips, the sides of reservoirs and sewage farms. They have increased and spread enormously in the last twenty years, and indeed the first pair only bred in Britain as recently as 1938. This increase parallels the growth and spread of gravel diggings. However as the Plovers require bare gravel and spurn most areas as soon as they get a

Figure 69 In its display fight the Snipe holds two of its tail feathers stiffly out almost at right angles to its body. They vibrate as the bird rushes through the air producing a musical whirring or 'bleating' sound.

covering of vegetation, the presence of breeding pairs at one particular pit may only be for a period of a few years after the original excavation.

Once the eggs are laid the nesting waders become much more secretive, and it is often difficult to know whether they are nesting unless one chances to come very close to the nest. When this happens, the birds indulge in a distraction display as described in Chapter 2. It is probably not a good idea to sit quietly to watch the incubating bird back on to the nest, as in most cases it will refuse to return while anyone is within sight, and during this period the eggs can chill or a predator may get them.

Migrant waders at inland fresh waters are rarely very numerous, with under 10 of any one species the rule at most smaller waters. Sometimes, though, flocks of several hundred waders may drop in and these are almost certainly on passage and unable to continue because of poor weather. There are quite regular migrations of waders right across the country, from the Wash to the Severn, or the Humber to the Mersey or Morecambe Bay, or from the Forth to the Clyde. So perhaps it is not so surprising when what one would normally regard as coastal species sometimes land beside some inland site. Dunlin, Knot, Grey Plover and godwits can all appear a long way inland.

The more common fresh-water migrant species are Greenshank, Spotted Redshank, and Green and Wood Sandpipers. They are all adept at using the cover of vegetation, walking around the edges of the water, pecking their insect food from the shallows and out of the mud. Most appear in the months of March to May and again from August to October. It is quite probable that individuals visit certain waters in successive years, but whether the same birds visit both in spring and autumn is not known. Certainly the species themselves are very regular in the same places each year.

Gulls

The Common Gull and the Black-headed Gull breed beside fresh-water wetlands in the north of England and Scotland, and have both been spreading inland in recent years. They build their nests on tussocks of rush or grass growing in and around the shallow bog pools on moorland, or in reedbeds around larger lakes. They use the water as a defence against predators, frequently feeding many kilometres away. Both species have a small territory around their nest which they defend from the intrusion of other gulls. This usually involves noisy calling with the head and neck bent low, bills wide open. Pairs also display a great deal to each other, continuously reinforcing the pair bond. When a pair have successfully driven off an intruder they nearly always return to their nest and indulge in what has been aptly termed a 'triumph ceremony', when they call eagerly at each other, heads held up, celebrating their victory.

Almost all the different species of gulls sometimes feed beside fresh water, though more usually nowadays they are at rubbish tips, sewage farms and other areas with an abundance of human waste. The larger gulls swim on the water, pecking at anything floating. In the case of the larger gulls, Great and Lesser Black-backs and Herring Gulls, they scavenge on dead fish or other large items. Black-headed Gulls eat quite a lot of insects and small items and are adept at picking them off the surface without actually landing. They hover momentarily by turning into the wind, dropping their feet until they just touch the surface and then seizing what they are after in their bills. This particular feeding method is much used at sewage farms where the birds may not want to soil their plumage by landing on the liquid. It can also be observed at gravel pits and reservoirs when perhaps the birds find more food items this way than by swimming. They should certainly be able to see them more clearly from above.

The habit of roosting on reservoirs and pits by gulls has greatly increased in recent decades and is now commonplace in many parts of the country. The birds generally disperse to feed during the day, on fields, rubbish tips and the like, flighting out in the morning and returning in the evening. Their likeness to geese in their use of the V-formation has already been mentioned. Having no shooters to fear, they flight out in broad daylight and return well before dark. Roosting gulls are not always looked upon favourably, as they have been accused of possibly introducing disease into drinking-water reservoirs, particularly perhaps when they repair to them direct from rubbish tips!

Figure 70 Two Black-headed Gulls feeding on a rubbish tip. Several kinds of gull now get much of their food from such tips, perhaps producing a health-hazard when they spend the night on the nearest drinking-water reservoir.

From the roost, the gulls disperse following a number of fairly consistent flight lines. Following these will lead to where the birds are feeding, and if this is done at intervals through a winter, a picture can be built up of the locations of the birds' principal food sources and how these may vary over a period of months. A large complex of roosts may require several people to investigate it thoroughly, but a single fairly isolated roost can be easily studied by one or two people.

Terns

Only the Common Tern regularly breeds beside inland fresh waters, choosing shingle-covered spits and islands. These have been successfully provided for them in some areas, or, where the water is too deep to build an island, shingle-covered rafts have been floated out. Even quite small rafts have been used for nesting by the terns. They seem not to mind a gentle rocking motion to their nest, in return for the complete safety from ground predators.

Terns are renowned for the fearlessness with which they defend their nests. The attacks are more potent when the birds are breeding in a crowded colony, but even a few birds can put on a considerable defensive display. The birds use the straightforward and very effective technique of dive-bombing any intruder, swooping down from above and either striking at the head or swishing by very closely. This attack is carried out on foxes, dogs, cattle, horses and humans. Whether the intruder is an active predator, merely a straying animal whose feet might crush the eggs, or someone out for an innocent walk, the answer is always the same. The attacks are sometimes quite painful, as the bird may hit one's head with its feet and additionally deliver a sharp peck with its pointed bill. At the same time it keeps up a piercing screech. Most animals are repelled by such attacks and stay away from the nests, the object of the exercise, and it requires some effort of will to keep walking in the face of such vigorous attention.

Migrant terns are frequent inland during the spring, when Black Terns, especially, appear at many waters in southern England. They are on their way to breeding grounds in the Netherlands and other parts of Europe, and every so often birds stay on in England and hopes are raised that they might breed. This has happened once in recent years but conditions have to be just right, with shallow floods over marshy, well-vegetated ground, and it is a matter of luck that the birds will find just what they require.

Feeding terns are a pleasure to watch. They have a light, very buoyant

Figure 71 The Lapwing nests some way from water, out in pastures and arable fields. It will bring its young to wet places and water margins where there is plenty of insect food.

Figure 72 A Little Ringed Plover returning to its well-camouflaged eggs. This species first bred in Britain in 1938 and has since spread to most of England aided by the great increase in gravel workings which provide ideal nest-sites.

Figure 75 One adult Common Tern is feeding a chick while its mate stays on the nest incubating unhatched eggs or brooding other chicks. This is the only tern species to nest regularly inland in Britain.

flight and swing to and fro, beating over the water, every so often dropping down to pick up a morsel from the surface, without more than a slight interruption to their flight. An alternative feeding method often used is to hover with the head held down looking into the water, and then make a quick, shallow dive to catch a small fish. Where there are shoals of small fry close to the surface, several terns may gather. Some indication of the efficiency of this method may be gathered by watching to see how often a bird is successful in its dive.

Swallow, martins and swift

For the aerial insect eaters of this group, water is a great provider of food, though not an exclusive one. All four species, Swallow, House and Sand Martin and Swift, feed almost entirely on insects caught in flight. They can feed anywhere there are insects in the air, and at times this can be many hundreds of metres up in the sky, on insects swept upwards by rising air currents. Frequently, though, they are drawn to the low-flying insects which hang in dancing clouds over water bodies, especially in the evenings. The majority of these are made up of mayflies. The males form the dense swarms, waiting for females with which to mate. The numbers involved are truly vast, especially as any one male mayfly probably only lives a matter of hours or at most a day or two. As the clouds apparently last for weeks at a time, the abundance of the insects is simply staggering. It is not surprising, therefore, to find the insect-

Figure 73 The Greenshank is another migrant visitor to fresh waters. It prefers open expanses of exposed mud where it can probe for food with its long bill. It will also wade in shallow water.

Figure 74 The Green Sandpiper is a common migrant to inland fresh waters, and small numbers winter in the southwest of Britain. They can be flushed from the sides of large lakes and reservoirs, and from quite tiny streams and ditches.

eating birds gathering to feed on them. All the species do this, though the Swift perhaps the least. Even if the insects cannot be seen, the presence of the feeding birds indicates where they are, whether it be low over the water, or higher up but still in the shelter of some trees, over patches of weed, and so on.

The Sand Martin is the only species which nests regularly beside water, in sand banks, on the sides of gravel pits and even in piles of washed sand beside the workings. They also use dry sites, in quarries and railway cuttings. They are opportunistic breeders, moving in very quickly if a potential new site is created, just as they can as rapidly lose a site if a new quarry face is dug, or the pile of washings carted away.

In the north of England and Scotland, the winter floods frequently

Figure 76 The parent Sand Martin is clinging to the side of the nest-hole while two of its chicks beg for food. Sand Martins nest in colonies in sand cliffs, often in temporary piles of gravel washings.

create clean, new river banks in which the birds can nest, but in the south the gentler flows produce graded, overgrown banks which are unsuitable; hence the use of gravel pits. The only more or less permanent Sand Martin colonies can be found where they have adopted soil drainage pipes protruding from river banks.

When a colony is discovered it is often very difficult to estimate its size. Merely counting the number of holes is unlikely to give the right answer, as old holes persist from previous years and some burrows are dug but not used. Birds also land at and enter burrows other than their own, adding to the confusion. Indeed later on in the season young birds of the first brood may move to other colonies and roost in spare holes, while the breeding adults are busy on the second family of the summer. In the autumn Sand Martins gather in large roosts, often in beds of low willow or reeds, at times in their tens of thousands.

Although House Martins are probably most often seen breeding on the sides of houses, right into the centre of towns, they do sometimes breed on bridges over rivers as do Swallows. Both species use mud in the construction of their nests, coming down to wet patches and puddles to gather the small pellets and take them back to their nests. A recently exposed muddy area at the side of a lake is an ideal site for them.

Figure 77 House Martins nest commonly under house eaves often well away from water. However, they must come to water, if only to a puddle, in order to find mud for nest-building.

Kingfisher

Often the first indication one has of the presence of a Kingfisher is the loud, shrill 'chee-chee' call, given as the bird flies fast and low over the water. Indeed one wants to be extremely alert as soon as the call is heard, as the bird often gives only fleeting views as it speeds away. This is especially true on streams and canals where it will quickly be out of sight round the next bend. On lakes and gravel pits, at least it usually has to travel further, which gives more chance of a good view. It is not always appreciated that Kingfishers also have a song, a series of high-pitched but varied whistles, delivered in rapid succession on the wing. The period when they sing is not very long, from mid-May to the end of June, but it is well worth listening out for. The bird flutters into the air, flying rather like a large butterfly, showing off its brilliant colouring, whistling all the while.

If the song is one way of attracting a female, the male Kingfisher also indulges in furious aerial chases in which other birds may join. Where Kingfishers are common, it is not impossible to see five or six birds flying in fast pursuit, often climbing well above the water, even amongst trees. Sometimes the whole group of birds ceases its chasing and settles in the upper branches. A further type of display by the male, to impress

Figure 78 A Kingfisher leaving the water with a large fish in its bill. The bird will return to its perch, usually an overhanging bough, and kill the fish by beating its head against the wood, before swallowing it head first.

his mate, is to fly in tight figures-of-eight or circles.

Kingfishers dig their own nest tunnels, a nearly horizontal passage running back from the entrance for as much as a metre, to end in a hollowed-out chamber. The initial digging of the hole is done by the bird flying at its chosen piece of vertical river bank, endeavouring to cling to the face while probing with its bill. As soon as a small depression has been created the bird can hold on properly and start the serious digging. The short legs and feet are not digging tools but are used to shuffle the soil out backwards and expel it from the hole. Observing a hole being dug is difficult; the birds resent intrusion, and where possible will always use a previous year's hole, perhaps just cleaning it out and repairing it. They do not use any nest material, laying their eggs on the bare ground. Fish-bones have been found in excavated chambers but these are probably the remains of food taken in for the young ones.

As with other fish-eating birds which catch their prey by diving into the water, the Kingfishers are by no means successful every time they dive. If one can get into a position to watch a feeding bird, it is worth checking just how many dives it makes in order to catch one fish. The best time to watch this is when the pair are feeding young and the hard-pressed parents are fishing as much as they can.

Dipper

The wonderful ability of the Dipper to move around underwater was described in Chapter 2. Dippers are typically birds of fast-flowing rivers and streams, but can also be found on more lowland waters, including canals. In some areas they also inhabit the margins of the larger lakes, particularly in northern England and Scotland. They are sedentary

Figure 79 A Dipper perched on a boulder with a beakful of stoneflies and their nymphs. Most of the Dipper's food is obtained underwater where it manoeuvres skilfully with the aid of its wings.

birds, leaving their home only in very cold weather. During both summer and winter the pair or a single bird will defend a territory, a length of stream or a section of a lake shore. Walking along such a stream, if one flushes a Dipper it will move ahead of you until it reaches the limits of its territory. It is very reluctant to leave it and so will then double back, flying round in an arc in order to regain the stream in its own patch.

Dippers call with a metallic 'chink-chink' but this is often difficult to hear against the noise of rushing water. So too is their song, a pleasant trilling warble, not so unlike a Wren's, but rather sweeter and less urgent sounding. It is mostly delivered when the bird is perched on a boulder, or sometimes a tree branch, but sometimes a flying bird will utter it too. Dippers do not, though, indulge in wild aerial chases during courtship, like the Kingfisher. Instead the pair bow and bob to each other, quivering the wings, and singing and calling.

The Dipper's nest is almost invariably placed over water, which provides security from predators reaching the nest. The structure itself is a deep cup of moss, leaves and other vegetation, with a domed roof built over, if the space chosen allows. Almost any ledge or support will do: a gap in brickwork under a bridge, ivy clinging to a wall or tree, a natural ledge under a waterfall or in a gully, or just the support of a tree branch. Even when the site of the nest is apparent from the visits of the adults feeding their young, it can be almost impossible to approach closely, so well situated is it for this necessary protection.

Wagtails and pipits

These are waterside birds, rather than waterbirds. The Pied and Grey Wagtails are the species most closely tied to water, the former occurring in a wide variety of habitats, the latter restricted to fast-flowing streams in the summer though descending to lowland waters in the winter. Both species build their nests on ledges of one kind or another, on walls, in ivy against tree-trunks and so on. Whereas the Pied Wagtail may nest far from water, however, the Grey Wagtail is invariably close to it, often in a situation where running water washes the foot of the wall or bank. The Grey Wagtail is one of those species which actually seems to prefer Man's artefacts for its nests in preference to a natural site such as a bank or tree. Old walls, culverts, bridges, locks and the like are chosen far more than any other kind of site.

Outside the breeding season it is rare to see Grey Wagtails in other than very small numbers, often still in pairs. Most are sedentary though there is some movement to lower ground in hard weather. Pied Wagtails, on the other hand, have large roosts which they use through the winter. Traditionally these are in reedbeds and other thick vegetation close to water, but not always large sheets. The dense growth beside a tiny village pond has, in one case, held several hundred birds. In recent years there have been cases of Wagtail roosts forming in the trees along

Figure 80 Pied Wagtails breed beside fresh water of all kinds, feeding on insects collected from the ground or caught in the air. Winter roosts of several hundred birds or more occur in reedbeds, trees or even inside glasshouses.

suburban roads and even inside buildings such as glasshouses which have roof vents open. If a roost is found, the birds can be watched flying in as dusk falls, usually coming in small parties and from several directions. When a thousand birds or more gather in one small area it is an unusual spectacle to say the least, and quite noisy, with the constant calling 'chissick' as they drop into cover. This soon quietens though and one is left wondering where all the birds have come from, because it is quite rare to see flocks of more than 20 or 30 Pied Wagtails feeding together during the day. The catchment area for the roost must be quite large.

The migrant Yellow Wagtails, too, gather in reedbed roosts in the autumn, prior to their departure for Africa. Generally they choose quite large stands of reeds and are not as conspicuous as the Pied Wagtails. Yellow Wagtails breed in wet fields and marshy places in the southern half of England, but in much drier habitat further north, including moorland and cultivated fields.

Pipits, particularly the Meadow Pipit, may sometimes be seen feeding on insects beside fresh water. They too nest in low-lying damp fields in some districts, though also in very much drier situations. The Water Pipit is the only species habitually found by fresh water, and then only as a winter visitor. Its close relative, the Rock Pipit, breeds around our coasts and is replaced inland, particularly in stony mountainous areas of Europe, by the Water Pipit. The most likely place to see the Water Pipit in England is on one of the chalk stream watercress farms of the southern counties. They walk and hop along the rows of cress, picking up insects from the leaves and out of the water.

Figure 81 Yellow Wagtails are migrants to Britain and Europe, wintering in Africa. They breed in wet meadows and may gather in autumn flocks to roost in dense reedbeds.

Warblers

The chattering songs of Reed and Sedge Warblers rise from most large patches of reeds, the latter species also spreading along overgrown ditches some distance from open water. The birds are insect eaters, only able to spend the summer in Britain and migrating to Africa for the winter. They are not conspicuous birds, preferring to remain hidden from view, even when singing. The most that is often seen is a small brown shape flitting through the reeds, the multiple stems preventing a clear view of the whole bird. Occasionally they emerge to sit near the top of a reed stem, gripping it, one foot above the other and swaying with the wind.

It is not advisable to plough through reedbeds trying to get better views of these warblers, or to seek their nests. The songs are sufficiently different to permit relatively easy identification if the birds cannot be seen well enough. While both are essentially chattering warbles, the Sedge Warbler's song includes a great many scratchy notes, together with high-pitched squeaks, while the Reed Warbler has a much more even, sweeter range of notes. Both possess a certain rhythmic quality, a kind of double beat on each phrase, especially the Sedge Warbler.

In autumn, some of the larger reedbeds, particularly on or near the south and east coasts of Britain, become the assembly points for warblers preparing to depart for the south. Sedge and Reed Warblers are probably the commonest species, but Whitethroats, Blackcaps and Willow Warblers also move in, coming in search of food. Before embarking on a major flight which may take them several hundreds of kilometres they need to put on fat as an energy source on the journey. Reedbeds provide this energy in the form of dense swarms of aphids, the common greenfly.

Figure 82 The Sedge Warbler sings to attract a mate and announce the presence of its breeding territory. Although commonly breeding in reedbeds, Sedge Warblers also nest along ditches and streams with thick vegetation.

The growing shoots of the reeds become thickly coated with the tiny insects, sucking away at the juices inside. The warblers could hardly have an easier feeding place and consume very large quantities. They need to, of course, as a Sedge Warbler may increase its weight by 60 to 70% in the course of a very few weeks. Some years, presumably because of poor weather, there are few aphids present. The warblers then have to spread out into the surrounding countryside for food and have a much harder time finding enough.

Buntings

The Reed Bunting is the only member of this mainly seed-eating family to be associated with fresh water. Its nest is built on the ground or slightly raised up in thick vegetation. The conspicuous male, with his black cap and white neck mark below it, is frequently seen sitting on the tops of reeds, or flying over them. Reed Buntings are a very sedentary species, wandering only a little in winter.

The male Reed Bunting marks out his territory in the spring by singing from a prominent perch, up above the general level of the vegetation. The need for a perch is so important that the presence of a suitable one may dictate whether there are, for instance, two territories

Figure 83 A male Reed Bunting singing on a prominent perch in his territory. The territory size and shape may be governed by the number of available perches. The song is a series of 'tseek' notes, beginning slowly and increasing to a trill.

in an area, or only one. If there are two willow trees or bushes projecting above a fringe of reeds on a lake side, then two Reed Bunting territories can be formed; just one tree may mean that only a single Reed Bunting male will be present. The territories and the necessary song perches can best be studied during a walk along a river in the spring. The singing males will be very prominent, and their position can practically be predicted by noting the locations of possible perches for them. Where there is an abundance of perches then the territories will be quite even in size, and at the optimum length of river to provide the necessary food for parents and young. Where trees are sparse, the territories may be uneven in size, depending on the distance between possible perches.

5 Studying the birds of inland fresh waters

There are a number of ways in which the birdwatcher can contribute meaningful information about the birds he sees, in addition to the sheer pleasure to be had from firstly identifying and then watching the birds. National organisations like the Wildfowl Trust and the British Trust for Ornithology (see Appendix II) run surveys and regular monitoring schemes, gathering information from all over the country. Local natural history and ornithological societies also carry out local censuses and studies. And then there is ample scope for contributions to knowledge based on careful or regular observations at one site or on a particular bird or species.

The Wildfowl Trust, whose headquarters are at Slimbridge in Gloucestershire, has been running a National Wildfowl Count Scheme for over 30 years which provides information on the numbers and distribution of all the different species of wildfowl throughout Britain. Amateur birdwatchers are requested to count the numbers of wildfowl on their local lake, reservoir, stretch of river, estuary or length of coast, once a month from September to March. The monthly count dates always fall on the Sunday nearest to the middle of the month. Forms are provided either direct from Slimbridge or through a local organiser covering a county or region and these are returned at the end of each winter.

Counting birds is not particularly difficult, provided the numbers are not too large. Flocks of ducks swimming on the water are fairly straightforward if they number several hundreds or even a thousand or two. There are rather few places in Britain where the ducks number many thousands and they are usually large areas covered by a team of people rather than an individual. Where the birds are reasonably spread out and not moving very much, then the best technique is to scan across the flocks using binoculars or a telescope and either to count each individual bird or estimate them in fives or tens. With a really large flock it is very easy to lose one's place and also to forget which number has been reached. A telescope on a tripod enables the counter to move steadily through the flock from one side to the other. Remembering where one has got to in the totals is harder, but if it becomes a real problem, one can purchase a small hand tally counter quite cheaply and press a small button every ten birds, say, and look at the total indicated when the counting is finished.

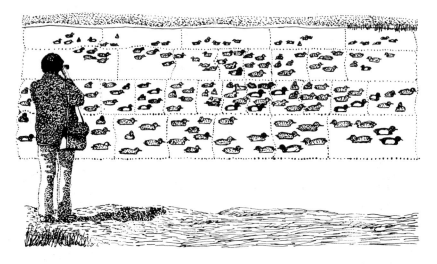

Figure 84 Estimating numbers of birds on the water is relatively straightforward provided the birds are not moving too much. Counting in fives is often possible, with a high degree of accuracy.

Not all birds will sit quietly to be counted, of course, with diving ducks and birds in flight being the hardest to assess. A flock of Tufted Duck or Pochard which is feeding busily is almost impossible to count accurately. At any one moment half or more of the flock may be underwater and as one counts through the flock so birds pop up and disappear even as one tries to number them. A rather drastic solution is to scare them into stopping feeding for a while, though this is very difficult if the birds are far away, and anyway not a solution to be encouraged. The only safe method is to wait until they have stopped feeding by coming back a few hours later, or trying a different time of day.

Flying birds have to be counted quickly and here estimating has to be adopted. The usual method is to count quickly ten, 20 or even 100 birds, as accurately as possible, and then to estimate what is in the rest of the flock on the basis of the approximate area taken up by the sample just counted. It is perhaps a little crude but can be surprisingly accurate, especially with some experience. Ideally, of course, the flock settles and allows a careful, accurate count. If this does happen be sure to spare the time to count the birds again; a check on the previous estimate is both more useful as a count and also enables one to judge the correctness of the estimate and so gain confidence for next time.

At the individual site level, the regular wildfowl counts provide a picture of the numbers of the different species using a lake or reservoir. Set in the national context, the site can be rated as of local or regional importance, or, if it carries substantial numbers of a particular species,

Figure 85 Estimating numbers of birds in flight is often difficult, as it has to be done rapidly. A small flock can be roughly grouped in tens, but larger flocks may require blocking off into 50s or even 100s. A hand tally counter becomes an invaluable aid at such times.

it may be thought to be of national or even international importance. A fairly widely adopted method of rating sites has been to say that if a site regularly holds one per cent of the total population of a particular species, then it is of international importance. Similarly if it holds one per cent of a national population, then it is of importance at the national level. This may seem fairly arbitrary but for most species it does result in a realistic number of sites being so graded, and between them those sites usually contain a good proportion of that species or population.

The aim of such counts of course, is to ensure adequate protection for the different species and populations. By listing the national and internationally important sites for the different countries of northwest Europe, it is possible to achieve more effective conservation and protection measures than if each country tried to look at its birds in isolation, perhaps using different criteria.

The information on the individual sites is stored on a computer at Slimbridge and can be called up at will. It is not only the large internationally important sites which may warrant attention. Applications to

NATIONAL WILDFOWL COUNTS
THE WILDFOWL TRUST
SLIMBRIDGE, GLOUCESTERSHIRE

Several observations on the SAME water may be recorded on this Form. Please enter the dates at the head of each column, and any remarks and comments on the local conditions on the back of the form.

COUNTY: ESSEX

EXACT LOCALITY: ABBERTON RESERVOIR   NEAREST VILLAGE OR TOWN: COLCHESTER

NAME and ADDRESS of REPORTER:

A. COUNTER,
17, NEW ROAD,
COLCHESTER,
ESSEX.

DATE	15/9 /1980	13/10 /1980	17/11 /1980	15/12 /1980	13/1 /1981	16/2 /1981	16/3 /1981
MALLARD	4698	2338	709	1333	2043	1081	392
TEAL	5237	478	419	547	467	20	28
WIGEON	283	95	2	1270	2652	3550	905
PINTAIL	56	14		2			
SHOVELER	202	852	358	171	174	63	43
POCHARD	201	369	1412	402	650	215	12
TUFTED	2065	1982	1837	1706	1021	686	548
GOLDENEYE	1		66	230	426	344	422
GOOSANDER	1			20	18	16	12
MERGANSER							
SMEW							
GADWALL	164	104	181	198	69	184	85
SHELDUCK		6	1			2	61
GREYLAG	35						
WHITEFRONT							
BEAN							
PINKFOOT							
BARNACLE							
BRENT							
CANADA	55			32	75		36
MUTE SWAN	59	28	22	32	32	20	45
WHOOPER							
BEWICK					1	41	
GT. CRESTED GREBE	17	19	19	21	23	11	10

sail on reservoirs, to drain marshes, or to water-ski, all affect the wildfowl populations of the particular water. By using the information from the Wildfowl Count Scheme it is possible to provide a balanced picture of the numbers actually using that site together with information on where the birds might go if displaced by some other activity and whether the numbers are important in a local, regional or international context. Clearly if one of a group of gravel pits is turned over to sailing, it is probable that the displaced birds will move to a neighbouring pit and there will be little or no overall loss. If a large isolated reservoir is under the same threat, however, then the effect on the birds would be that much greater, as the whole area would lose its wildfowl. The count scheme does not then concentrate solely on the most important sites but tries instead to cover the complete spectrum from the very large reservoirs to the smallest lakes.

Apart from information on individual sites, the wildfowl counts provide data on the populations of the different species of wildfowl. There are few species for which the counts can provide complete censuses resulting in anything approaching a count of total numbers. What they are doing in the main is giving a count of a reasonably large sample. Using these it is usually possible to make a fairly intelligent guess at the total population. Thus for the Teal, which are found in fairly large flocks in a comparatively small number of places during the winter months, the total population has been estimated to be about 75,000 at peak. This is likely to be accurate to within 10 per cent. But for the Mallard, which is very widespread and occurs on all types of water from large reservoirs to the smallest ponds and ditches, the figure of 300,000 that has been suggested is little more than an educated guess.

Although it is important to have some idea of how many of each species of wildfowl occur in Britain, the main purpose of the wildfowl counts is to provide an idea of the trends that may be taking place in the numbers. By comparing the numbers of birds present one winter with those present the next, it can be seen whether populations are moving up or down. Clearly one has to adopt certain rules, by comparing the same sites and also counts made in the same months each year. So the number of Pochard, say, counted on 50 sites in November one winter can be compared with the number on those same 50 sites in the following November, and the year after, and so on. The pattern of change is built up in this way for all the different species, both nationally and regionally.

For some years a system of priority counts has been used to provide information on seasonal trends. About 200 waters were selected on the basis that they regularly carried good numbers of the commoner species, and the counters were asked to send in their counts as soon as they were

Figure 86 A form used for the monthly wildfowl counts organised by the Wildfowl Trust. The counter covers his local water on the middle Sunday of each month from September to March, sending in the form at the end of the winter.

made, and not to wait until the end of the winter. Comparing the numbers of birds on these selected sites month by month and year by year enabled the production of figures showing trends much earlier than if it had been left until all the counts had been received.

The overall information provided by the Wildfowl Count Scheme was used in a book on the status and distribution of British wildfowl some years ago (*Wildfowl in Great Britain*, HMSO, 1963). This has long been out of print, as well as out of date, and a completely revised version is being prepared and should be published in 1982.

It must be apparent that the Wildfowl Count Scheme could not operate without the continued help of many hundreds, or even thousands, of amateur birdwatchers. Approximately 800 waters around the country are counted regularly each month, while a further 600 to 700 lesser waters are covered once or twice each winter, coinciding with coordinated counts right across Europe.

Many of the same people also take part in complete censuses of wildfowl and other birds. Although it is well nigh impossible to count adequately every single site where the commoner ducks may be found, for some species with a more restricted distribution, it can be achieved. For example, most of the goose species occur in rather large flocks in relatively few places. The Pink-footed and Greylag Geese wintering in northern England and Scotland do so in a combined 100 sites or just a few more. Often the two species occur together. At the beginning of November each year, about 100 birdwatchers are circulated with a request to count the numbers of the two kinds of geese in their area, usually as they leave or arrive back at a roosting lake. The coverage is normally sufficiently good to enable the whole of both populations to be counted in the course of a weekend, to a total currently of about 80,000 in each.

Although there is much to be said for using the same counters year after year (they build up experience of their local conditions and thus should become more accurate in making their counts), naturally there is a turnover and new counters are also needed and very welcome. One way to join in is to contact one's local ornithological society and find out who is the area organiser of the counts. No great skills are needed beyond an ability to identify the different species and a willingness to count regularly month after month. And of course, while counting there is always the possibility of seeing a rarity or making some other exciting observation.

The other organisation which relies totally on amateur help in its

---

Figure 87 A colony of Black-headed Gulls beside a moorland pool. They have been spreading and increasing inland in recent years both as a breeding species and in winter.

Figure 88 A Sand Martin colony in the side of an old quarry. The birds re-use the same holes year after year as long as they remain intact but excavate new ones when necessary using their bill and claws.

surveys is the British Trust for Ornithology at Tring, Hertfordshire (see Appendix II). This body carries out a number of routine monitoring studies, like the wildfowl counts, though these are not specifically directed at fresh water, and it also organises short-term surveys directed at a particular species or object. Its largest such project, carried out between 1968 and 1972, was to map the distribution of all the breeding birds in the country, the results being published in *The Atlas of Breeding Birds of Britain and Ireland*, Poyser, 1976. In 1981 it is just beginning an equivalent survey to map the wintering distribution of birds. The breeding atlas required about 10,000 helpers and it is likely that the wintering atlas will need to be on the same scale.

Surveys directed at wetland birds have included regular censuses of breeding Herons and Great Crested Grebes, carried out every few years, and on the Little Ringed Plover, to monitor its spread across the country. Other recent projects have included regular counts through the summer of the numbers of different species breeding along inland waterways, rivers and canals, and an assessment of the impact of recreation on the birds of inland waters. This last survey was carried out mainly by the Wildfowl Trust, using the network of counters of the Wildfowl Count Scheme, and also involved the British Trust for Ornithology and its membership.

Nearly every county has a local representative of the British Trust for Ornithology, who is usually in close touch with the local birdwatching society. Censuses and surveys are organised through these representatives and volunteers are always welcome to take part. As explained, the involvement may vary from a single count once in a summer, to ensuring regular coverage of a site or species in a particular type of habitat. Thus birdwatchers of all degrees of experience and commitment can find something in which to take part.

So far I have examined various surveys on a large scale, to which each individual counter makes a small contribution. The value of these cannot be overestimated but at the same time the birdwatcher may want to extract more from his own records, or alternatively, there may not always be the time or the inclination to make regular observations on behalf of a national survey. In the last chapter a number of indications were given of where there are gaps in our knowledge, or information can be learned by a single observer making even sporadic counts or observations, though naturally, the more frequent and regular the better.

The first and essential requirement of any series of observations is that they are recorded properly and systematically. Contributors to national surveys are invariably supplied with printed forms to complete on a monthly or annual basis. The information requested on these is probably

Figure 89 A photograph taken with flash of a Dipper coming to its nest to feed its hungry young. The nest is almost always placed over water and under an overhang, typically a bridge or wall, but also under natural banks and in caves.

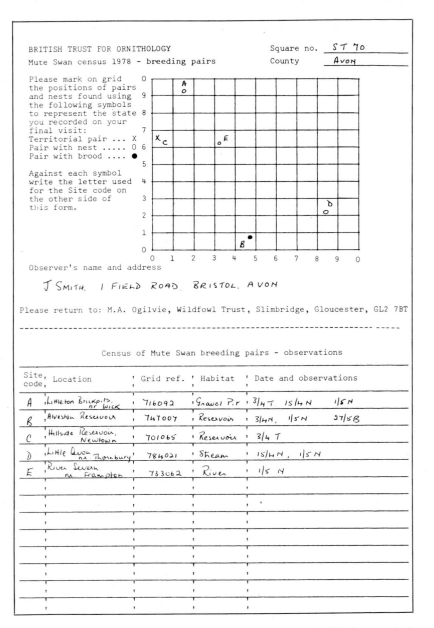

Figure 90 One of the forms used in a recent census of Mute Swans in Britain, organised by the author for the British Trust for Ornithology. The basis of the census was the 10 kilometre square of the National Grid, found on all Ordnance Survey maps. Observers were asked to note the positions of breeding and territorial pairs and to record the habitat, date of visit and so on.

Figure 91 This map shows the spread of the Little Ringed Plover as a breeding species in Britain, from its original first nesting in Middlesex in 1938. The species only occurs rarely in Ireland and has not yet bred.

the most that the organiser feels he can reasonably ask from all his counters. For one's own observations it is probably best to treat these as a minimum and to add any further details that seem both relevant and easy to record. It is very important to maintain the discipline of recording both background facts and the birds one sees, in as consistent a manner as possible. The relevance of some of the information may not always be apparent at the beginning of a study but then gaps in knowledge are often impossible to fill subsequently.

To begin with the obvious details to note are date, time of day, basic weather information, and one's route or position. The day of the week may be important, too, as disturbance is often much heavier at weekends. The behaviour of the birds varies markedly through the course of a day, particularly the times they are displaying or feeding. And obviously the weather influences many of their actions. If the water-level of the lake or reservoir varies a great deal, and it is simple to record these changes, then this should be done too. Many reservoirs have a visible depth-gauge, and it may be possible to construct one for a lake.

While the area of water may remain the same, changes in the immediate surroundings can have a marked effect on the birdlife. The felling of a sheltering belt of trees or the planting of new areas, the varieties of crops on adjacent fields and therefore the type and amount of farming activity as well as the availability of different foods before and after harvest, the creation or loss of other fresh waters in the neighbourhood (particularly important in gravel pit areas), are all likely to affect what goes on at any one water.

Counting is probably the simplest routine birdwatching to undertake, and its usefulness was stressed earlier. However such surveys as the National Wildfowl Count Scheme only request counts once a month from September to March. There is thus great scope for making more regular counts throughout the year. Weekly or twice-weekly counts through the autumn and winter will often detect considerable changes in numbers of certain species which do not show up in less frequent observations. For example, short-term fluctuations in numbers often indicate successive waves of migrants moving through an area, and over a period it may be possible to estimate not only how many birds use the haunt at any one time, but also how many use it during the course of a season or a year.

In the example shown in the table below, twice weekly counts of Mallard and Teal were carried out, including the monthly National Wildfowl Counts occurring on 15th September and 16th October. For Mallard, the latter fairly well represents the actual picture revealed by the more frequent counts. There was a steady increase through September reaching a level in early October which was maintained for the rest of the month. The Teal, on the other hand, clearly came through in two waves, one in late September following a rather slow build-up in the first part of the month, then another in late October. The monthly counts duly recorded an increase but missed the peak numbers. It is, of course, not always possible to calculate the complete turnover of birds, but at least one can arrive at a minimum number that must have visited and then moved on.

Twice-weekly Mallard and Teal counts in September and October

	Mallard	Teal		Mallard	Teal
Sept			Oct		
1	260	110	2	375	310
4	260	170	6	400	260
8	280	170	9	450	300
11	320	200	13	460	325
15	340	225	16	450	325
18	340	410	20	450	350
22	335	450	23	460	490
25	320	485	27	450	460
29	350	525	30	450	365

Counting of waterbirds is usually restricted to the winter months because that is when peak numbers are present in the country. Only small numbers of most species breed in Britain and apart from occasional surveys these tend to be less well monitored. However, counting pairs of grebes and ducks in spring and females with broods later in the summer, can produce interesting information on, for example, the colonisation of newly-created waters. This is especially true of gravel pits, and indeed studies of how these gradually acquire vegetation and birds evolving from bare gravel and plantless water into mature well-inhabited haunts can be fascinating.

In recent years counts of wildfowl in the summer have revealed considerable flocks of moulting birds arriving on certain favoured waters in June and July and staying for several weeks. For example there are now flocks of up to 2,000 Tufted Ducks on some of the London reservoirs each summer. These are almost certainly not local birds but immigrants from the breeding areas round the Baltic and even further east. The flocks are composed almost entirely of males, which have deserted their mates once the clutch has been laid, and some females which have probably failed to breed. They leave the breeding grounds and seek suitable waters on which to spend the period of the annual wing-moult when they become flightless for a few weeks. Such waters must have plenty of food as the birds will be incapable of moving to find more until their new wings have grown and they can fly again. The London reservoirs clearly fulfil this requirement. The discovery of these flocks and the monitoring of their increase to the present substantial numbers was the work of an amateur birdwatcher working entirely in his spare time.

Some of the birds which feed in and over water, and which may breed right beside it or some distance away, can also be monitored by

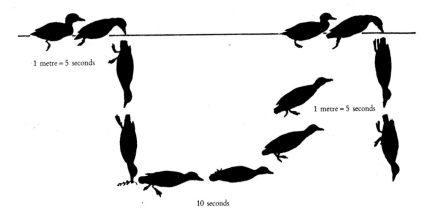

1 metre = 5 seconds

1 metre = 5 seconds

10 seconds

bird dives and pauses, dives and pauses 25-40 times and then rests 5 to 10 minutes before starting once again

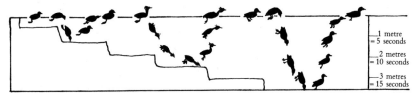

1 metre
= 5 seconds

2 metres
= 10 seconds

3 metres
= 15 seconds

Figure 92 A diagram to illustrate how timing the dives of birds can give information on feeding habits and the depth of water for example.

counting them at the waterside. Herons are censused regularly in Britain by counts made at their nesting colonies. It is not usually possible to ascertain how many young are reared in the tree-top nests, but young birds can be distinguished in the autumn by their lack of the adult head-plumes. Thus at a water where Herons are regular visitors, the number and proportion of young birds each autumn can be compared. The nesting sites of Sand Martins may be changed from year to year, particularly in areas of gravel pits where new digging may wipe out a previous colony location. Watching for the birds feeding may often give a clue to the whereabouts of colonies, as well as a crude assessment of numbers.

For a birdwatcher seeking a straightforward project, the timing of the dives of the different species of underwater feeding birds is something which is very easy to do and of considerable interest. If one were to pose the question of how long the different diving bird species stay underwater on average, it would be possible to find a published figure for virtually all of them and some of these were given in Chapter 2. However these various figures come from a wide variety of sources, from several types of water, taken at different times of year, in varying weather, and so on. They are not really comparable at all. If one observer were to record systematically the diving times of several species on a single water, however, he could find real differences between species faced with the same conditions, as well as the variations which might take place through the course of a year in the diving patterns of the same species.

Some of the points to be looked for in a small study of this kind include a knowledge of the depth of the water in which the birds are diving. If the water is a reservoir the water authority will possess contour maps of the bottom which can be used. The average time a bird spends underwater is closely related both to the average depth of the water and, for example, whether it is feeding from the bottom. If the water is about one metre in depth, then if 20 seconds are spent underwater, perhaps five seconds are spent reaching the bottom, ten seconds searching for food, and a further five seconds coming up to the surface again. Fish-eating species will spend all the time underwater searching for and chasing their prey, and the diving times should be linked with the approximate distance travelled, though this can be difficult to estimate.

Feeding dives of some species are frequently broken up into bouts of perhaps 30 to 40 dives, one after another with very short breaks in between, which may last a half to a third as long as the average length of the dives themselves. There is then a rest period of a few minutes before another bout of diving. Such a pattern is quite characteristic of the grebes for example. Some of the diving ducks appear to bob up and down more frequently for shorter periods before resting. This behaviour may be correlated with how much food they are finding.

Thus if on every visit to a lake the diving times of different species are recorded and related to where they are feeding, a useful picture can be built up of comparisons between the species in a way which is rarely done, simple though the exercise is. This is just one example, and there are many others, where an observer can contribute to our knowledge of birds, with no more skill and equipment than a pair of binoculars, perhaps a watch or stopwatch, and the ability to identify the birds. It is a great mistake to think that everything is known about birds and their behaviour. It is not true, and probably never will be, even about some of the commoner species.

Other questions posed in previous chapters include, how often Kingfishers are successful in catching a fish when they dive into the water, whether newly arrived migrant birds, particularly storm-blown vagrants, put in more time feeding soon after they arrive rather than later, if there is any relationship between wind speed and direction and Cormorants 'drying' their wings, whether your local swans breed equally well each year by bringing the same number or proportion of young birds with them, if the same goose leads the skein all the time it is within sight, where the gulls which roost on your local gravel pit are feeding, and if these locations change through the winter, how far the House Martins which are feeding over the water are coming from their breeding sites, and many more.

Many birdwatchers like to add to their observations by taking photographs. This may develop into a more consuming passion than birdwatching itself, and so fall outside the scope of this book. However, the camera can be used as an additional tool in bird study, rather than just to obtain portraits at the nest, or of birds swimming or walking, which normally requires the use of hides and spending long hours in them. Unfortunately most wetlands are rather flat and large, and do not lend themselves particularly well to photography. However, a single-lens reflex camera with a modest telephoto lens of 135 or 200 millimetres focal length, can be used to take pictures of displays, or of flocks, which can then be studied or counted at leisure.

Counting birds from photographs used to be done from black-and-white prints but these are restricted in size and it is much easier to use colour transparencies. If a transparency is projected and therefore enlarged onto a large sheet of paper, a mark can then be made with a pen or pencil on each bird shown, and these can be counted and checked. There are two drawbacks to using photographs for counting birds. Firstly it may not be possible to identify all the birds correctly in mixed flocks. Secondly, and more importantly, it is essential that the photograph includes all the birds in the flock. It is too late to go back and take another picture if it is discovered that the first one has chopped off part of the flock!

Much can be learnt about birds by catching and ringing them. In Britain the British Trust for Ornithology runs the national ringing scheme, organising the training of ringers, the issuing of rings, the keeping of records, and so on. Full details can be obtained from the BTO (see Appendix II). Apart from general studies of migration and mortality, ringing birds consistently at one site, perhaps linked with individual marking with colour rings, provides a basis for many very interesting and detailed studies of all kinds of birds.

Before one can become a ringer and have one's own rings, it is necessary to undergo a period of training with an experienced ringer, usually lasting two or three years. This is best done by joining a group of ringers and learning the various techniques of catching birds, the correct way of handling and ringing them, and the way in which to keep the necessary records. The welfare of the birds is paramount and so it is important to ensure that new ringers entering the scheme are totally competent in every respect. Working in a group of ringers does, in fact, have many advantages as it usually means that there are sufficient resources in catching equipment and manpower to carry out fuller studies than would be possible by someone working on their own.

The principal method of catching small birds is the mist net. These are made of very fine-mesh black nylon or terylene, and are suspended between tall poles. A typical mist net is about two metres high and from 20 to 60 metres long. It is divided along its length into three or four panels by taut strings. The netting is slack enough to form pockets over these

Figure 93 Terylene mist nets used to catch birds for ringing. Warblers and other small birds moving through the rushes fail to see the fine meshes and get caught in the pockets of loose netting hanging over the taut horizontal strings.

strings and it is into these pockets that the bird falls after colliding with the almost invisible net. Its feet, and sometimes its head and wings, get lightly tangled in the netting, and the bird then normally lies quietly until released by the ringer. It is one of the rules of mist netting that nets are inspected frequently on a regular basis so that the time a bird is held in the netting is kept to an absolute minimum. These nets are particularly suitable for using in thick cover, such as reedbeds, where they catch Reed and Sedge Warblers, Reed Buntings and wagtails. Out in the open they become more visible but even so can catch Swallows, martins and Swifts, especially when these are feeding low over the ground.

The larger waterbirds require more elaborate methods of capture. Some of these have derived from traditional techniques used to trap birds for the market. The duck decoy is probably the single most successful method of catching ducks. There are five of them in use in Britain at the present time, all catching ducks for ringing. They are the last survivors of over a hundred which existed from the seventeenth to nineteenth centuries, mainly on the east coast. They were a Dutch invention and brought over to this country in the seventeenth century.

Figure 94 A duck decoy being worked. The decoy man sends his dog in between the overlapping reed screens while he remains out of sight. The ducks follow the dog, perhaps thinking it is a fox, and are eventually flushed into a narrow keeping net. Formerly used to catch birds for the market, decoys are now used for ringing.

Essentially a decoy consists of a secluded pond between a quarter and one hectare in extent. It has several arms of water, usually four or eight, leading away from the main pond, each curving out of sight over 40 or 50 metres. They are covered with hoops bearing netting and gradually taper over their length from three to six metres wide and high at the mouth to a narrow end of perhaps 50 centimetres where there is a detachable net or basket for removing the birds. The ducks are attracted into the pipes, as the arms of water are called, either by food spread in the water and along the banks, or because of the tendency of waterfowl to follow and mob a predator. So a brown collie, or other dog resembling a fox, is trained to run along the sides of the pipes appearing and disappearing behind reed screens which line each pipe, shielding the human presence from the birds on the pond. The ducks, intrigued by this vanishing 'fox', swim into the pipe to see where it has gone to and to mob it if it reappears. Once several birds are well under the hoops of netting, the decoy man appears at the mouth of the pipe and flushes them right to the far end where he can extract them. Catches of several thousand ducks have been made in a winter in many decoys, formerly all for the market, but now at least for ringing and release.

Although one or two old decoys have been renovated in Britain in

Figure 95 A large cage trap in shallow water in a reservoir. Dabbling ducks find their way inside through narrow funnels to feed on grain with which the trap is baited. They cannot find their way out and are removed for ringing and release to study their movements.

recent years, no one is likely to build one from scratch just to catch ducks for ringing. The most usual alternative method is to use large cage-traps, simple structures of wire-netting on a wooden frame, perhaps two metres square and a metre-and-a-half high. These are placed at the edge of the lake or reservoir, protruding into shallow water. At the water level are small funnels leading into the trap, which is baited with corn. The ducks swim in, feed themselves, and then cannot find a way out, because the funnels end near the centre of the trap, and the birds automatically swim to the edges seeking an escape.

For many ringers the idea was once to put rings on as many birds as possible and then sit and wait for recoveries which would show where the birds had moved to. In this way routes, timings and distances of migration were discovered for a variety of species. Nowadays, however, there is a much greater emphasis on more detailed studies, though the recoveries, especially if from far-distant places, lend an added interest. By trapping regularly at one site, particularly if about the same amount of effort is put into the catching each day or weekend, in terms of the amount of hours spent catching and the numbers of nets or traps used, information can be built up on the use of the area by different species and even by individuals. The length of time birds remain in an area, the use they make of it, perhaps for feeding though nesting elsewhere, the proportion returning in subsequent years, and many other aspects can be discovered. Not only do these findings tell one more about the birds, they are also valuable in helping to assess the importance of the particular site to the birds.

Knowledge of the birds at individual sites, gathered from counting, ringing and other studies, has been used to produce assessments of the

Figure 96 Canada Geese, like all other wildfowl, become flightless for a few weeks in summer when they moult their wing feathers. At this time they can be rounded up and driven into a netting pen for ringing.

conservation value of all important localities in this country. Among fresh-water wetlands, a number have been made into reserves, protecting them from damaging developments of any kind, though many more still need protection. The Nature Conservancy Council (see Appendix II), the government conservation body, has several National Nature Reserves covering wetland areas. Some of these, such as Rostherne Mere, Cheshire, have hides for birdwatchers, though at others it is necessary to obtain a permit first. It is mainly the voluntary national and local conservation bodies which have done most to establish reserves with access for birdwatchers.

The Wildfowl Trust has reserves on the Ouse Washes, at Welney, Norfolk, and beside its wildfowl collection at Martin Mere, Lancashire, where there are several hides overlooking the best spots. The hides are usually provided with seats, conveniently placed rests for the elbows, and in some cases glassed-in windows rather than the more normal, but also cold and draughty, wooden shutters, whose opening and closing often scares birds very close to.

The Royal Society for the Protection of Birds (see Appendix II) has a fine network of reserves all over Britain, including many covering areas of inland fresh water. Nearly all of them have wardens who guide visitors round and help them to identify birds, as well as carrying out necessary management work to maintain and improve the habitat on the reserves. Among the more important RSPB reserves are a further area of the Ouse

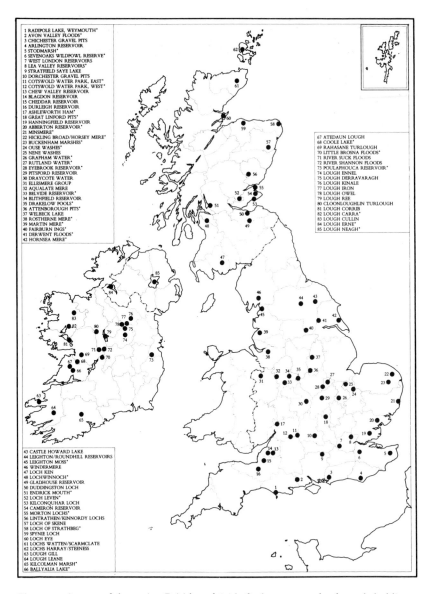

1 RADIPOLE LAKE, WEYMOUTH*
2 AVON VALLEY FLOODS*
3 CHICHESTER GRAVEL PITS
4 ARLINGTON RESERVOIR
5 STODMARSH*
6 SEVENOAKS WILDFOWL RESERVE*
7 WEST LONDON RESERVOIRS*
8 LEA VALLEY RESERVOIRS*
9 STRATFIELD SAYE LAKE
10 DORCHESTER GRAVEL PITS
11 COTSWOLD WATER PARK, EAST*
12 COTSWOLD WATER PARK, WEST*
13 CHEW VALLEY RESERVOIR
14 BLAGDON RESERVOIR
15 CHEDDAR RESERVOIR
16 DURLEIGH RESERVOIR
17 ASHLEWORTH HAM*
18 GREAT LINFORD PITS*
19 HANNINGFIELD RESERVOIR
20 ABBERTON RESERVOIR*
21 MINSMERE*
22 HICKLING BROAD/HORSEY MERE*
23 BUCKENHAM MARSHES*
24 OUSE WASHES*
25 NENE WASHES
26 GRAFHAM WATER*
27 RUTLAND WATER*
28 EYEBROOK RESERVOIR*
29 PITSFORD RESERVOIR
30 DRAYCOTE WATER
31 ELLESMERE GROUP
32 AQUALATE MERE
33 BELVIDE RESERVOIR*
34 BLITHFIELD RESERVOIR
35 DRAKELOW POOLS*
36 ATTENBOROUGH PITS*
37 WELBECK LAKE
38 ROSTHERNE MERE*
39 MARTIN MERE*
40 FAIRBURN INGS*
41 DERWENT FLOODS*
42 HORNSEA MERE*

67 ATEDAUN LOUGH
68 COOLE LAKE*
69 RAHASANE TURLOUGH
70 LITTLE BROSNA FLOODS*
71 RIVER SUCK FLOODS
72 RIVER SHANNON FLOODS
73 POULAPHOUCA RESERVOIR*
74 LOUGH ENNEL
75 LOUGH DERRAVARAGH
76 LOUGH KINALE
77 LOUGH IRON
78 LOUGH OWEL
79 LOUGH REE
80 CLOONLOUGHLIN TURLOUGH
81 LOUGH CORRIB
82 LOUGH CARRA*
83 LOUGH CULLIN
84 LOUGH ERNE*
85 LOUGH NEAGH*

43 CASTLE HOWARD LAKE
44 LEIGHTON/ROUNDHILL RESERVOIRS
45 LEIGHTON MOSS*
46 WINDERMERE
47 LOCH KEN
48 LOCHWINNOCH*
49 GLADHOUSE RESERVOIR
50 DUDDINGSTON LOCH
51 ENDRICK MOUTH*
52 LOCH LEVEN*
53 KILCONQUHAR LOCH
54 CAMERON RESERVOIR
55 MORTON LOCHS*
56 LINTRATHEN/KINNORDY LOCHS
57 LOCH OF SKENE
58 LOCH OF STRATHBEG*
59 SPYNIE LOCH
60 LOCH EYE
61 LOCHS WATTEN/SCARMCLATE
62 LOCHS HARRAY/STEENESS
63 LOUGH GILL
64 LOUGH LEANE
65 KILCOLMAN MARSH*
66 BALLYALIA LAKE*

Figure 97 A map of the major British and Irish fresh-water wetlands, each holding a regular peak of more than 1,500 wildfowl. Waters only used as roosts by geese are excluded. An asterisk indicates that at least part of the site is protected.

Washes, near the Wildfowl Trust reserve, Radipole Lake, Weymouth, Hornsea Mere, Humberside, on the south side of Loch Leven, Kinross, Loch Strathbeg, Grampian, and Leighton Moss, Lancashire. A full list, with visiting details, can be obtained from the RSPB.

County Naturalists Trusts (see Appendix II) all have reserves, sometimes, though not always, smaller than those of the national bodies. A recent listing of them will be found in *The Birdwatcher's Year Book*, edited by J E Pemberton.

Among many private reserves is the Sevenoaks Wildfowl Reserve. Visitors are welcome and should write to the Warden, Bradbourne Vale Road, Sevenoaks. Some examples of the fascinating management of the gravel pits which make up the reserve are given in Chapter 6.

Visiting any of these reserves can be very enjoyable. There are often more birds and a greater variety to be seen than at other sites; the birds are easily viewable from the hides and the wardens can tell visitors much of interest concerning the specialities of the reserve. Some birdwatchers may be involved in setting up a reserve, having contributed their local knowledge in ensuring its conservation. Others become members of local support groups, providing voluntary wardens on busy days, helping in active management and assisting the warden in recording the birds. This kind of help is welcome at nearly all reserves, and very rewarding for the participants.

6 The conservation of inland fresh waters and their birds

Looked at overall there is no shortage of fresh water in Britain; perhaps as much as one per cent of the total area of the country is fresh water of some kind. Yet much of this, such as large, deep highland lochs, is unsuitable for birds, and the pressures on the rest are immense. A few hundred years ago there was much more fresh water in some areas and much less in others. Before the extensive drainage of the fens of East Anglia, many square kilometres of marshes provided a haven for water-birds of all kinds. Until less than a hundred years ago almost all the lowland rivers of Britain had extensive floodplains in their lower reaches providing extensive wetlands where now there is farmland. Against these losses, though, must be set the many reservoirs and gravel pits which have been built or excavated in all parts of the country, but especially the populous southern half, where both the water and the excavated minerals have been required.

It is not possible to make realistic estimates of the numbers of the different species of waterbirds that used to exist in Britain, before so much drainage was implemented and other changes were made. What is more certain, however, is that species liking wet, marshy ground, such as Bewick's Swans, Wigeon and Redshank, have been losing habitat, while diving ducks like the Tufted Duck and the Pochard have far more than there used to be.

However a newly created reservoir or gravel pit is not always to the total advantage of the birds. The pressures from people wanting re-creational outlets have been growing steadily in recent years. Sailors, fishermen, water-skiers, walkers and birdwatchers all want the use of waters, and, alas, not all their demands are compatible, either with each other or, more especially, with the birds that also want to use the water.

There was something of an explosion in waterborne recreation in the 1960s and early 1970s. Before that many drinking-water reservoirs were strictly controlled as to access. Even birdwatchers had to have permits and in some cases were not allowed even to walk along the water's edge for fear of contamination. There were some exceptions, of course, but on the whole the larger reservoirs were *de facto* bird sanctuaries. The need for more and more areas for sailors and fishermen led to a government directive instructing water authorities to consider allowing some kind of recreation on their waters. Quite quickly it was found that people could be allowed in, and enjoy themselves, without any ill-effects to the water

Figure 98 Sailing is one of the most popular of water sports. Birds will not tolerate boats coming too close but if bays and sheltered areas are set aside for them, they will be able to share the water with the boats.

quality. But not, alas, to the birds. The presence of large numbers of sailing boats, or motorcraft towing water-skiers, or even contemplative fishermen lining the banks, makes any water much less attractive to them. Few species will tolerate boats close to them on the water, and while fishermen on the banks will not affect birds in the middle of a large lake or reservoir, some species need to come ashore to rest or to brood their young, and this could become impossible.

As the various waters were opened up, so the conservation bodies

Figure 99 Electronic flash stops the movement of this Kingfisher in flight allowing the brilliant colouring to be seen to perfection. The large powerful bill contrasts with the comparatively small feet which are only used for perching, never for holding fish.

Figure 100 A Grey Wagtail at its nest. The chicks are nearly ready to fly and have retreated off the nest and into the cover behind. These birds are resident on lowland streams but may leave their upland haunts in winter.

tried to resist in order to protect the most important sites. The main problem they faced, and still do, is that the water authorities, who own the reservoirs, have discovered that there is an income to be had from allowing people to use reservoirs for recreation. Sailors and fishermen will pay considerable sums in rent or day permits in order to practise their sport. Birdwatchers, on the other hand, whilst prepared to pay something, can rarely match the sums involved. A sailing club might pay the water authority several thousand pounds a year, but can equally draw on the subscriptions of several hundred members as well as obtaining grants from the Sports Council towards the provision of club houses and other facilities. For the sailing club members this may be their only outlet for their sport, and they are prepared to devote quite a lot of money to it. Birdwatchers, on the other hand, pursue their hobby in many different places and while prepared to spend a few pounds on a permit to allow them to visit a particularly good site, cannot collectively match the sums raised by other sporting interests.

If sailing is started on a comparatively small water, then most if not quite all of the waterbirds will be driven away. On the really large reservoirs, however, there may still be room for at least some of them to stay. There have been some interesting compromises worked out at some of these sites whereby several different recreations can take place at once. The concept of 'multi-use' of a reservoir developed slowly as a possible answer to the conflict of interests that had arisen. It has not always worked out well in practice, but there are now several examples from which suitable lessons can be drawn so that future attempts are managed to best advantage.

At the Chew Valley reservoir in southern England, when sailing was introduced the conservation bodies protested loud and long. The reservoir was one of the best in the country in terms of the numbers and variety of waterbirds, both breeding and wintering, found there. Fishing was allowed, though strictly controlled, both from the banks and from a limited number of boats. But this did not conflict with the birds very much. Then it was proposed that sailing should be allowed. This was considered a disaster by the conservation bodies and they did not hesitate to say so. However, it became clear that the water authority concerned was not prepared to concede that their reservoir might be important to the birds as such. The only response they made was to ask how many birdwatchers regularly came to the reservoir. On learning that it was probably in the order of 250, the active membership of local societies, their reply was to point to the several hundred fishermen who bought permits each year, and the sailing club, already formed to take over the concession, with 400 members and still growing, which was prepared to pay an annual rent of thousands of pounds. It just was not possible to

Figure 101 A Reed Warbler at its nest in the reeds. The main structure of the nest is built between the reed stems, while the upper part includes material woven round the reeds from which it is all suspended.

get them to make any allowance for the fact that the numbers of ducks using the reservoir made the site of national if not international importance for wildfowl. It was people and what they could pay which they considered more important.

There were many discussions, of course, and finally a compromise solution was worked out. The area in which sailing was permitted was restricted to the deeper water of the reservoir, to a total of rather less than half the surface area. The extensive shallows, small bays and the neighbourhood of an island, all very important to the birds, were kept free of boats at all times. In addition fishermen were not allowed along some of the banks so that complete sections of the reservoir were kept free of all disturbance. The birdwatchers, formerly able to walk at will right round the reservoir, were also restricted, except for a very small number of permit holders carrying out censuses and other studies. Instead hides were erected by the water authority so that better views could be had than hitherto of some of the best bays and inlets. The water authority also made one other significant concession; another, rather smaller, but still important reservoir not far away, also under their control, would not have any sailing on it, though fishing would continue.

The result has been quite satisfactory for all. The numbers of birds have dropped a little, and perhaps as overall in the region most species were increasing, the loss has been greater, but for a few species the reservoir is as attractive as ever and it still remains a very important water for birds. Local birdwatchers still get splendid birdwatching, if not quite with the freedom they once had. On the other hand, the water authority, the sailors and the fishermen are all much more aware than they once were of the value of the reservoir for birds, and the importance that the birds command.

Not all experiments at multi-use have been so successful. At another large reservoir where it might have been assumed there was room for all

Figure 102 Fishing is less disturbing to birds than sailing, but boats out on the water and fishermen standing at frequent intervals round the banks can scare many birds away.

interests, the birdwatchers got squeezed almost out of sight. This was a greater pity as it was a new reservoir and there should have been time during the planning stages to build in the necessary arrangements for successful multi-use. The problem seemed to be that the sailors and fishermen were both more definite in spelling out their requirements and more successful in winning the necessary arguments. Thus, although two shallow inlets were designated from the start as a nature reserve area where birds and other wildlife would be encouraged, and a birdwatching hide was built, the fishermen managed to gain access for fishing from the banks of the reserve area, while the sailors, although normally prevented from sailing into the reserve, won permission to do so during competitions and on special occasions when a longer reach of water was required.

The reserve was therefore only a partial success as the numbers of birds remaining on the water was probably considerably less than might have been the case had a larger, or better protected reserve been created. This is not to say that it was a total loss, or a waste of time trying; there are still more birds present than there would have been if there were no reserve at all.

These two case histories have provided useful lessons which have been applied elsewhere in the country and will be applicable in the future, too. Anyone involved in discussions on the establishment of a reserve area, or in resolving a possible conflict with other interests, should visit other waters where more than one recreation takes place and see what lessons there are to be drawn. In this way, although there have been overall losses for the birds in the last 20 years, future losses can be minimised or even prevented altogether.

There are now very few natural fresh waters in the southern half of Britain. Floods along rivers have been largely eliminated by drainage schemes in order to improve the land for farming. Marshes are virtually a thing of the past. The few floodland areas which do remain are nearly all under threat of drainage and some have only been protected after considerable efforts have been made. Outright purchase by a conservation body is usually the only real safeguard and even then some drainage plans can overrule the wishes of the owners.

Safeguarding what exists is one necessary facet of conserving our wetland habitat, but an increasing amount of experience and information on improving it so that it will hold greater numbers and a wider diversity of species has also been gained. If there are likely to be less and less fresh-water areas available solely for birds, then it makes sense to increase the value of what remains. Some policies are large-scale and expensive to carry out, but there are many things which can be done by a small group of people without large resources. Even a small increase in the number of birds on a water, or the number of pairs breeding, must be worthwhile.

A newly dug gravel pit is only barely hospitable for birds. The shores are devoid of much vegetation, the banks are steep-to and exposed, and

Figure 103 Declaring a gravel pit as a reserve is only the first step. Active, carefully planned management is then needed to exploit the full potential of the area and create optimum habitat for the greatest possible variety and number of birds.

there is often much rubbish in and around the water. The classic example of improving a gravel pit for birds is that of the Sevenoaks gravel pits, where the work was largely inspired and directed by the late Dr Harrison. The details of the work and the results in terms of increased numbers of all kinds of waterbirds have been written up and published but a summary of the more important successes and how they were achieved is given here, relating them to other types of water where this is appropriate.

The topography of the pit is of vital importance in determining the extent to which it will attract birds. In Chapters 1 and 2, the overriding value of an island as a nesting site for ducks and other species was mentioned. When management work first started at Sevenoaks there were no islands in the existing two lakes, but the gravel extraction company agreed, at no small expense to themselves, to leave an island about 15 × 8 metres, in a third lake then being excavated. In shallower pits there are often islands of spoil left behind when digging is finished, but it is as important with these, as with the specially created Sevenoaks island, that they are the right shape and profile. An island is of no use if the banks are vertical as no birds will be able to walk out of the water and make use of it. If the island is a mere rectangle or circle, it will be of much less value than if it is heavily indented to form separate little bays. An ideal shape is in the form of a cross, or perhaps a horseshoe. In this way separate discrete areas will be created, reducing conflict between several birds wishing to use the island, and one side or another will always have a sheltered bay whatever the direction of the wind. As well as having sloping banks it is important to keep at least some of the flatter areas free from vegetation so that they can be used for loafing. Other areas should

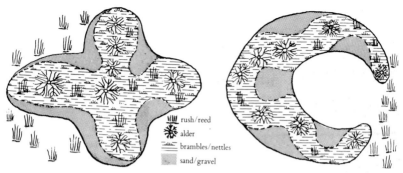

rush/reed
alder
brambles/nettles
sand/gravel

Figure 104 Islands provided for nesting birds in gravel pits or lakes should have a good mixture of vegetation growing on them, and be shaped to produce the maximum length of shoreline. Shelter from the prevailing wind should also be a consideration.

be planted with thick plants and low bushes to provide concealed nesting sites.

Much the same improvements in the way of detailed topography and vegetation can be made to the shores of the gravel pit. For example a dead straight shore, as so often left behind by the digger, is of limited value. Where possible it should be scalloped and indented to form many small bays with intervening spits. Each of these can be used by a female duck rearing her brood, providing shelter, food and freedom from interference by neighbours. It might seem a great labour to provide better habitat like this, but, for example, it may prove possible to dump a load of spoil out into the water to create a spit, and a spit automatically has a small bay on each side. Repeat that several times at intervals of some metres and a scalloped shore is quickly formed. Alternatively the spit can be cut off subsequently to form a small island with a sheltered channel between it and the bank.

Whatever topographical changes are made in this way, the rapid planting of them with the correct plants is vital. From studies of what the birds were eating, it was possible to plant up the Sevenoaks pit with those plants which it was known provided food that the birds liked. For example seed-bearing trees and shrubs like alder, birch and bramble not only provide food but also good shelter. Water plants like bur-reed, water dock, bulrush and various sedges are all seed-bearing and grow in thick stands in shallow water, thus giving additional shelter and nest-sites. Willows grow quickly and provide wind-breaks along exposed shores. Almost all the plants which one can find growing naturally around the shores of a lake will benefit a newly dug gravel pit if planted there.

Plants growing entirely in the water are also worth putting down, the various pondweeds, for example, which provide food for adult birds and also attract numerous aquatic insects which in turn will be food for ducklings. They also encourage the build up of muddy areas on top of

Figure 105 Bare sand-spits are important as daytime resting or 'loafing' areas for many species of wildfowl, especially the dabbling ducks. Good management may first create them and is then required regularly to keep them clear of encroaching vegetation.

the bare gravel.

The overriding aim of any scheme to improve a wetland for birds must be to provide the maximum variation in the habitat. Islands, shallows, spits and bays, tall trees, low shrubs, water plants in, growing out of and above the water, and so on. If the banks are flat and featureless, consider excavating shallow pools in them and dumping the spoil in low mounds. As these develop vegetation or are planted, so they add to the diversity of the area and to its potential to attract birds. Shallow pools, however small, beside the main lake will attract wading birds which might otherwise find the water inaccessible. Another way of providing an area for waders is to create an extremely shallow area that is exposed through any natural changes in the water level which may occur. Some gravel pits have areas of washings which have been dumped, producing the necessary shallows; in others they may be created.

Clearly, scope varies enormously according to local circumstances and resources. If there is an amenable gravel operator still working the area it may be possible to get major earthworks carried out. But if this sort of help is not available, then just planting and more modest adjustments to the topography are within the scope of any keen group of people and the results can be extremely rewarding. At Sevenoaks, for example, the numbers of wildfowl using the lakes grew enormously, and out of all proportion to changes in numbers taking place over a wider area. In ten years the use of the area by ducks, measured by the

Figure 106 Shallow pools with irregular shores and small islands form ideal breeding and feeding habitat for waterbirds. This area was artificially created within a gravel pit complex, and planted with rushes and other good food plants.

numbers of birds times the number of days they were counted, went up by six to eight times. More and more species appeared, some staying to breed, others on passage in an area where previously there was nothing for them.

The main techniques described above make use of nature by planting the right vegetation, altering the topography, and so on, but Man's technology can also help. Where there are no islands and no possibility of creating natural ones with spoil, then it is possible to construct rafts which form a more than adequate substitute. In a sense the larger they are the better they will be, but even a small construction, two or three metres by half that, is large enough for a pair of Great Crested Grebes to nest on or a pair of Coot. At Sevenoaks, rafts about three by four metres were made, based on watertight metal tanks and joined by lengths of metal strap and hawser. A shallow lip is needed round the rim, then topsoil is placed inside and suitable cover plants sown. Attached to a secure anchor such a raft is rapidly accepted by the birds and can have loafing Mallard on it, almost within hours of being floated into position. One Sevenoaks raft held the nests of two Mallard, two Tufted Ducks and a Moorhen all within a week of being anchored out in the lake, which demonstrates their value and the need for nest-sites which existed there, as at any other islandless gravel pit.

Another type of raft is not planted but covered with shingle instead so as to attract breeding Common Terns and this has been successfully

Figure 107 A well-matured nesting raft anchored in a deep gravel pit. The absence of islands in gravel pits, so vital to the secure nesting of many waterbirds, can be simply overcome by the construction of rafts.

achieved. The terns will not breed where there is thick vegetation and so it is necessary to keep the raft clear of vegetation, either by gardening before each nesting season, or by having some impermeable layer within the shingle such as polythene, to prevent plants becoming rooted.

Opportunities to improve wetland habitats do not come everyone's way but at least the knowledge is there, the experience which can be built on, thanks to the hard work and dedication of the pioneers such as Dr Harrison. Britain's wetlands may have increased in surface area in recent

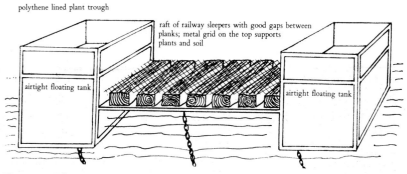

polythene lined plant trough

raft of railway sleepers with good gaps between planks; metal grid on the top supports plants and soil

airtight floating tank

airtight floating tank

Figure 108 The construction of a nesting raft.

years but the amount available to birds has probably decreased and will continue to do so. Thus every square metre must be managed to hold as much as possible. And every birdwatcher can play a part. This does not have to take the form of actively wielding a spade or pick, but can just as readily be done by making useful observations on which to assess the current importance of a water, and the use that the birds are making of it. Without a clear demonstration of the need for wetlands by the birds and other wildlife that lives on them, there will be little success in the battles necessary to preserve them. This is where everyone can assist, and help the birds and themselves in bringing increased pleasure and knowledge to their birdwatching.

Appendix I Scientific names of birds mentioned in text

Arctic Tern *Sterna paradisaea*
Bearded Tit *Panurus biarmicus*
Bewick's Swan *Cygnus columbianus*
Bittern *Botaurus stellaris*
Black-headed Gull *Larus ridibundus*
Black-necked Grebe
    Podiceps nigricollis
Black Tern *Chlidonias niger*
Black-throated Diver *Gavia arctica*
Canada Goose *Branta canadensis*
Chiffchaff *Phylloscopus collybita*
Common Gull *Larus canus*
Common Sandpiper *Actitis hypoleucos*
Common Scoter *Melanitta nigra*
Common Tern *Sterna hirundo*
Coot *Fulica atra*
Cormorant *Phalacrocorax carbo*
Dipper *Cinclus cinclus*
Dunlin *Calidris alpina*
Eider *Somateria mollissima*
Gadwall *Anas strepera*
Garganey *Anas querquedula*
Goldeneye *Bucephala clangula*
Golden Plover *Pluvialis apricaria*
Goosander *Mergus merganser*
Great Black-backed Gull
    Larus marinus
Great Crested Grebe *Podiceps cristatus*
Great Northern Diver *Gavia immer*
Green Sandpiper *Tringa ochropus*
Greenshank *Tringa nebularia*
Green-winged Teal
    Anas crecca carolinensis
Greylag Goose *Anser anser*
Grey Plover *Pluvialis squatarola*
Grey Wagtail *Motacilla cinerea*
Heron *Ardea cinerea*
Herring Gull *Larus argentatus*
House Martin *Delichon urbica*
House Sparrow *Passer domesticus*
Kingfisher *Alcedo atthis*
Knot *Calidris canutus*
Lapwing *Vanellus vanellus*
Lesser Black-backed Gull *Larus fuscus*
Little Grebe *Tachybaptus ruficollis*
Little Ringed Plover *Charadrius dubius*

Long-tailed Duck *Clangula hyemalis*
Mallard *Anas platyrhynchos*
Meadow Pipit *Anthus pratensis*
Moorhen *Gallinula chloropus*
Mute Swan *Cygnus olor*
Osprey *Pandion haliaetus*
Oystercatcher *Haematopus ostralegus*
Pied Wagtail *Motacilla alba*
Pink-footed Goose
    Anser brachyrhynchus
Pintail *Anas acuta*
Pochard *Aythya ferina*
Ptarmigan *Lagopus mutus*
Purple Heron *Ardea purpurea*
Red-breasted Merganser
    Mergus serrator
Red-crested Pochard *Netta rufina*
Red-necked Grebe *Podiceps grisegena*
Redshank *Tringa totanus*
Red-throated Diver *Gavia stellata*
Reed Bunting *Emberiza schoeniclus*
Reed Warbler *Acrocephalus scirpaceus*
Ringed Plover *Charadrius hiaticula*
Ruddy Duck *Oxyura jamaicensis*
Sand Martin *Riparia riparia*
Scaup *Aythya marila*
Sedge Warbler
    Acrocephalus schoenobaenus
Shoveler *Anas clypeata*
Slavonian Grebe *Podiceps auritus*
Smew *Mergus albellus*
Snipe *Gallinago gallinago*
Spotted Crake *Porzana porzana*
Spotted Redshank *Tringa erythropus*
Swallow *Hirundo rustica*
Swift *Apus apus*
Teal *Anas crecca*
Tufted Duck *Aythya fuligula*
Water Pipit *Anthus spinoletta*
Water Rail *Rallus aquaticus*
Whitethroat *Sylvia communis*
Whooper Swan *Cygnus cygnus*
Wigeon *Anas penelope*
WillowWarbler *Phylloscopus trochilus*
Wood Sandpiper *Tringa glareola*
Yellow Wagtail *Motacilla flava*

Appendix II Useful addresses

Army Birdwatching Society, c/o Lt. Col. N. Clayden, MOD Defence Lands, 4 Tolworth Towers, Surbiton, Surrey.

British Birds, c/o Fountains, Park Lane, Blunham, Bedford MK44 3NJ. This journal is produced monthly for birdwatchers; it includes papers on identification, biology and distribution, as well as notes, up-to-date birdwatching news and many photographs.

British Ornithologists' Union, c/o Zoological Society of London, Regent's Park, London NW1 4RY. This is the senior ornithological society in Britain. Members receive the quarterly journal *Ibis* and can attend scientific conferences.

British Trust for Ornithology, Beech Grove, Tring, Herts HP23 5NR. Members receive a newsletter six times a year and the quarterly journal *Bird Study*. The BTO coordinates the ringing scheme in Britain and Ireland, as well as issuing licences, nets, rings and other ringing equipment. Ringers receive *Ringers' Bulletin* and *Ringing and Migration* twice a year. The BTO also organises national surveys, including the Common Bird Census, the Waterways Bird Survey, and many others. It holds two or three conferences a year.

County Naturalists' Trusts. These own and manage reserves and organise meetings and outings for members. Addresses are available from local libraries or by sending an s.a.e. to The Royal Society for Nature Conservation, The Green, Nettleham, Lincs LN2 2NR.

Freshwater Biological Association, The Ferry House, Far Sawrey, Ambleside, Westmorland. Members receive an annual report and copies of scientific publications, and may visit the laboratories and use the library.

Irish Society for the Prevention of Cruelty to Animals, 1 Grand Canal Quay, Dublin 2.

The Irish Wildbird Conservancy, Southview, Church Road, Greystones, Co. Wicklow, Ireland. Members receive a regular newsletter. An annual conference is held jointly with the RSPB alternating between the Republic of Ireland and Northern Ireland. The IWC owns and manages several reserves.

The Irish Wildlife Federation, c/o 8 Westland Row, Dublin 2. Members receive newsletters. The IWF arranges lectures for its members and educational programmes for teachers and school children on birds and all aspects of conservation.

Nature Conservancy Council, 19 Belgrave Square, London SW1X 8PY, or see telephone directory for local and regional offices. Manages National Nature Reserves for which permits to visit can be obtained in most cases.

Royal Air Force Birdwatching Society, c/o Sq. Leader D. Hollin, RAF Wyton, Cambs.

Royal Society for the Prevention of Cruelty to Animals, The Manor House, Horsham, Sussex RH12 1HG, or see telephone directory for local officers and centres. Gives advice and help on treatment of sick birds.

Royal Society for the Protection of Birds, The Lodge, Sandy, Beds SG19 2DL. Members receive the magazine *Birds* four times a year and have access to over 60 reserves throughout Britain and Northern Ireland, including many fresh-water wetlands. The RSPB provides local and national meetings and film shows; local members' groups organise outings.

Water Space Amenity Commission, 1 Queen Anne's Gate, London SW 1H 9BT. The amenity arm of the water industry producing the quarterly magazine *Water Space*. Although more concerned with sports and recreation it is also involved with wildlife on reservoirs, canals, etc., producing maps and reports on the subject.

Wildfowl Trust, Slimbridge, Gloucester GL2 7BT. Members receive the annual scientific publication *Wildfowl* and the twice yearly magazine *Wildfowl World*. They have free access to the Trust's waterfowl collections and reserves.

Young Ornithologists' Club, c/o RSPB as above. Members are bird-watchers up to the age of eighteen. They receive the magazine *Bird Life* six times a year and a regular newsletter. Local members' groups organise field trips, film shows and meetings.

Further reading

Identification guides to birds

Bruun, Bertel and Singer, Arthur. *The Hamlyn Guide to the Birds of Britain and Europe*. Hamlyn, 1970, rev. ed. 1978.

Hayman, P. and Burton, P. *The Bird Life of Britain*. Mitchell Beazley in association with the RSPB, 1976.

Heinzel, Hermann, Fitter, Richard and Parslow, John. *The Birds of Britain and Europe, with North Africa and the Middle East*. Collins, 1972.

Jonsson, Lars. *Birds of Lake, River, Marsh and Field*. Penguin, 1978.

Peterson, Roger, Mountfort, Guy and Hollom, P. A. D. *A Field Guide to the Birds of Britain and Europe*. Collins, 1954, 4th ed. 1979.

Saunders, David. *RSPB Guide to British Birds*. Hamlyn, 1975.

Birdwatching guides

Conder, Peter. *RSPB Guide to Birdwatching*. Hamlyn, 1978.

Gooders, J. *How to Watch Birds*. André Deutsch, 1975; Pan Books, 1977 (paperback).

Gooders, J. *Where to Watch Birds*. André Deutsch, 1967, rev. ed. 1974; Pan Books, 1977 (paperback).

Gooders, J. *Where to Watch Birds in Europe*. André Deutsch, 1970, rev. ed. 1974; Pan Books, 1978 (paperback).

Ogilvie, M. A. *The Bird-watcher's Guide to British Wetlands*. Batsford, 1979.

Wallace, Ian. *Discover Birds*. Whizzard Press/André Deutsch, 1979.

Reference books

Cooper, J. E. and Eley, J. T. *First Aid and Care of Wild Birds*. David & Charles, 1979.

Cramp, S. and Simmons, K. E. L. (Eds.) *Handbook of the Birds of Europe, the Middle East, and North Africa. The Birds of the Western Palearctic. Vol. 1 Ostrich to Ducks*. (Covers divers, grebes, Cormorant, Bittern and wildfowl.) Oxford University Press, 1977. *Vol. 2 Hawks to Bustards*. (Covers Osprey and rails.) Oxford University Press, 1980.

Flegg, J. J. M. *Binoculars, Telescopes and Cameras for the Birdwatcher*. BTO Field Guide, No. 14, 1972.

Hollom, P. A. D. *The Popular Handbook of British Birds*. H. F. & G. Witherby, 1952, rev. 4th ed. 1968.

Mead, Chris. *Bird Ringing*. BTO Field Guide, No. 16. 1974.

Metcalf, John C. *Taxidermy*. Duckworth, 1981.

Pemberton, John E. *Birdwatcher's Yearbook 1981*. Buckingham Press, 1980.

Richards, Michael W. *The Focal Guide to Bird Photography*. Focal Press, 1980.

Identification guides to life in fresh water

Freshwater Biological Association. Scientific publications by various authors which include keys to several invertebrate groups.

Haslam, Sylvia, Sinker, Charles and Wolseley, Pat. *British Water Plants*. Field Studies Council, 1975.

Mellanby, H. *Animal Life in Fresh Water*. Methuen, 1938, 6th rev. ed. 1963.

Muus, Bent, J. and Dahlstrom, Preben. *Freshwater Fishes of Britain and Europe*. Collins, 1971.

Whitton, Brian. *Rivers, Lakes and Marshes*. Hodder & Stoughton, 1979.

Biology and ecology of wetlands and wetland birds

Atkinson-Willes, G. L. (Ed.) *Wildfowl in Great Britain*. HMSO, 1963.

Axell, Herbert and Hosking, Eric. *Minsmere*. Hutchinson, 1977.

Brown, Philip. *The Scottish Ospreys*. Heinemann, 1979.

Eastman, Rosemary. *The Kingfisher*. Collins, 1969.

Fjeldsa, Jon. *The Coot and the Moorhen*. Av-media, Copenhagen, 1977. (Includes colour slides and cassette tapes.)

Harrison, Jeffrey. *The Sevenoaks Gravel Pit Reserve*. WAGBI, 1974.

Hutchinson, C. D. *Ireland's Wetlands and their Birds*. Irish Wildbird Conservancy, 1979.

Lack, David. *Swifts in a Tower*. Methuen, 1956.

Macan, T. T. *Freshwater Ecology*. Longmans, 1963.

Macan, T. T. and Worthington, E. B. *Life in Lakes and Rivers*. Collins, 1951; 1972 (paperback).

Murton, Ron. *Man and Birds*. Collins, 1971.

Nethersole-Thompson, Desmond and Maimie. *Greenshanks*. T. & A. D. Poyser, 1979.

Ogilvie, M. A. *Ducks of Britain and Europe*. T. & A. D. Poyser, 1975.

Ogilvie, M. A. *Wild Geese*. T. & A. D. Poyser, 1978.

Owen, M. *Wildfowl of Europe*. Macmillan, 1977.

Owen, M. *Wild Geese of the World*. Batsford, 1980.

Scott, Peter and the Wildfowl Trust. *The Swans*. Michael Joseph, 1972.

Sharrock, J. T. R. *The Atlas of Breeding Birds in Britain and Ireland*. T. & A. D. Poyser for the BTO and IWC, 1976.

Vaughan, Richard. *Gulls in Britain*. H. F. & G. Witherby, 1972.

Index

Page references in italic refer to illustrations; page references in bold refer to recognition details of birds in Chapter 3.

Acknowledgements

Colour photographs

Aquila: D. Green 17 top, G. R. Jones 36 bottom, A. T. Moffett 108 bottom, M. C. Wilkes 71 top and bottom; Ardea: J. A. Bailey 18, 107 bottom, I. Beames 53 top, Werner Curth 126, Kenneth Fink 17 bottom, David and Katie Urry 54 top, Richard Vaughan 35 top; Bruce Coleman: Leonard Lee Rue 89 top, John Markham 53 bottom, Roger Wilmshurst 72, J. van Wörner 89 bottom; David Hosking 35 bottom, 143 top; Nature Photographers: Derick Bonsall 144, Michael Gore 108 top, M. R. Hill 90 bottom, Chris Mylne 125 top, David Sewell 143 bottom, Roger Tidman 54 bottom, 107 top, Derek Washington 125 bottom; Royal Society for the Protection of Birds: Michael W. Richards 36 top; Bryan Sage 90 top.

Black-and-white photographs

Aquila: F. V. Blackburn 118, R. J. C. Blewitt 38, 82, S. C. Brown 40, D. Green 32, 85, E. A. Janes 115, J. Lawton Roberts 113, R. T. Mills 103, 117, 148, A. J. Richards 142, M. C. Wilkes 41; Ardea: F. Balat 31, J. B. & S. Bottomley 80, M. D. England 93, Ake Lindau 7, Wilhelm Möller 37, Richard Vaughan 97, 105, 111; Biofotos: Heather Angel 9, 11, 15, 16, 146; Frank Blackburn 42, 100; K. J. Carlson 44, 45, 110, 116; Bruce Coleman: Gordon Langsbury 86; Pamela Harrison 22, 23, 75, 87, 92, 101, 137, 150, 151, 152; David Hosking 96, 109; Eric Hosking 136; Nature Photographers: A. K. Davies 135, Paul Sterry 102; M. A. Ogilvie 138; Royal Society for the Protection of Birds: Hansgeorg Arndt 46, 77, 78, 95, Fritz Pölking 112, W. Suetens and P. van Groenendael 99.